Portrait of
Inequality

Portrait of Inequality
Black and White Children in America

Marian Wright Edelman
with research by Paul V. Smith

Copyright © 1980
by the Children's Defense Fund

All rights reserved

No part of this publication may be reproduced or transmitted in any form or by any means, electronic or mechanical, including photocopy, recording, or any information storage and retrieval system, without permission in writing from the publisher.

For additional copies or for information about the material
in this book:
Children's Defense Fund
1520 New Hampshire Avenue, N.W.
Washington, D.C. 20036

Library of Congress Catalog Card Number: 80-68585
Printed in the United States of America

ISBN 0-938008-00-5

This book is dedicated to M. Carl Holman, who has been a quiet teacher and doer for so many years.

It is also dedicated to Winson and Dovie Hudson and Mrs. Mae Bertha Carter. These unheralded Mississippi women have never stopped courageously standing up for children despite formidable obstacles and dangers. Their day-to-day grit is the model for the rest of us.

Preface

Portrait of Inequality differs from CDF's previous eight books in that portions are written in a personal tone. While the facts of unequal opportunity speak for themselves, many of the suggestions in the section "To Change the Portrait" reflect my own background—as a Black child who grew up in the segregated South, a college sit-in student, a civil rights attorney in Mississippi—and my views as a Washington-based lawyer for children grappling with how to translate the last two decades of experience, laws, and programs into positive daily realities for individual children and families.

I speak as one who believes deeply in the importance of strong family, church, and Black community support for Black children's well-being. These three factors bolstered me and many of my generation against the hostile external world that daily attacked and neglected us and sought to squash our aspirations. As we got older, adult role models like Martin Luther King, Jr., Whitney Young, Benjamin Mays, and Carl Holman were there to guide, nurture, and validate our young desires to break from the past and build a different future. How many more of these models our young people need today to navigate the labyrinth of narrowing opportunity in an era of shaky commitment to racial justice and growing economic scarcity. In emphasizing the importance of Black self-help, I also recognize that many Black families and children have no boots and cannot pull themselves up by their own bootstraps. Equally thoughtful leadership and targeted strategies are required on behalf of the Black child from the public and private sectors.

Like CDF's other publications, *Portrait of Inequality* lays out the problems but also attempts to say what ought to be done about them. In each of the areas discussed in the action agenda, CDF has staff, information, and a range of materials available to those interested in deepening their understanding of the problems of Black children and in pursuing any of the recommended actions. CDF's Children's Public Policy Network staff will work with local, state, and national groups interested in becoming more actively involved in children's issues. All are encouraged to participate in the network, to subscribe to its monthly newsletter, *CDF Reports*, or to use its toll-free line, (800) 424-9602. CDF's network staff also holds briefings for selected national and state leaders on a range of children's issues and is holding meetings in a number of states each year to encourage the creation of or to work more closely with existing state networks for children. Please let us know of your needs and interests. We are eager to work with you.

Marian Wright Edelman
President

Contents

Preface

Part I

Introduction	1
A Portrait of Inequality	7
To Change the Portrait	9
An Action Agenda for Black Children	20
Child Health	22
Child Care	26
Education	29
Youth Unemployment	33
Children Without Homes	36
Housing Discrimination Against Families With Children	40
Family Support and Services	42

Part II

Numbers of Black and White Children and Families		46
Table 1	Number of Children in the United States by Age and Race, March 1979	47
Table 2	Number of Families in the United States by Presence of Own Children under 18 and Race	48
Family Structure		49
Table 3	Percentage of Children by Age, Relationship to Family Head, and Race, March 1978	50
Table 4	Percentage of Children by Family Living Arrangement and Race, March 1979	51
Table 5	Percentage of Children Aged 6-17 by Family Living Arrangement and Mother's Marital Status and by Race, 1975	52
Table 6	Percentage of Children Living with Two Parents by Age and Race, March 1979	53

Poverty 54

Table 7	Median Income for Families and Unrelated Persons by Race, 1969 and 1977	56
Table 8	Median 1978 Family Income of Children by Family Type and Race, March 1979	57
Table 9	Per Capita Family Income by Family Type and Race, 1977	58
Table 10	Percentage of Related Children Living in Families with 1977 Incomes below the Poverty Level by Age and Race, March 1978	59
Table 11	Percentage of Related Children Living in Families with 1978 Incomes below the Poverty Level by Family Type and Race, March 1979	60
Table 12	Percentage of Related Children Living in Families with 1977 Incomes below the Poverty Level by Ages of Children in the Family, Family Type, and Race, March 1978	61
Table 13	Percentage of Related Children Living in Families with 1977 Incomes below the Poverty Level by Age of Family Head, Family Type, and Race, March 1978	62
Table 14	Percentage of Families with 1977 Incomes below the Poverty Level by Age of Family Head, Family Type, and Race, March 1978	63
Table 15	Number of Children and Families Receiving AFDC by Race, 1975	64

Unemployment 65

Table 16	Percentage of Children Affected by Parental Unemployment by Race, March 1979	66
Table 17	Percentage of Youths Aged 16-21 Who Are Unemployed by Sex and Race, July 1979	67

Table 18	Percentage of Youths Aged 16-24 Who Are Unemployed by Level of Education Completed and Race, October 1978	68
Maternal Employment and Child Care		69
Table 19	Percentage of Children Whose Mothers Work or Are Seeking Work by Age of Child and Race, March 1979	70
Table 20	Percentage of Children under 6 Whose Mothers Work or Are Seeking Work by Race and Family Type, March 1979	71
Table 21	Percentage of Children Aged 3-5 Attending Nursery School or Kindergarten by Age, Length of Day, and Race, October 1978	72
Table 22	Percentage of Children Aged 3-5 Attending Nursery School or Kindergarten Who Are in Full-day Programs by Type of Program and Race, October 1978	73
Education		74
Table 23	Percentage of Children by Family Type, Education of Family Head, and Race, March 1978	76
Table 24	Percentage of Black Public School Students Attending Majority Black Schools by Racial Composition of School and School Year	77
Table 25	Percentage of Public School Students Attending Schools with Enrollments of 90 Percent or More Same-race Students by Region and Race, School Year 1976-77	78
Table 26	Percentage of Children Aged 5-17 Enrolled in Lower Grades than Typical for Their Age by Age, Family Income, and Race, October 1976	79

Table 27	Additional Percentage of Black Students Who Miss Questions on Academic Achievement Tests by Subject and Age, 1971-1975	80
Table 28	Percentage of Public School Students in Special Education Placements by Type of Placement and Race, Fall 1978	81
Table 29	Ratios among Public School Special Education Placements by Race, Fall 1978	82
Table 30	Percentage of Public Elementary and Secondary School Students Disciplined during the 1977-78 School Year by Type of Disciplinary Action and Race, Fall 1978	83
Table 31	Percentage of Youths Aged 18-24 by Age, High School Enrollment Status, and Race, October 1978	84
Table 32	Number of School Dropouts and High School Graduates Aged 16-24 by Race, 1977-78	85
Table 33	Percentage of Children and Youths Aged 5-19 Not Enrolled in School by Age and Race, October 1978	86
Table 34	College Enrollment among Youths Aged 20-21 by Race, October 1978	87

Child Health 88

Table 35	Percentage of Live Births by Month in Which Prenatal Care Began and by Race, 1978	89
Table 36	Infant Death Rates in 1950 and 1978 by Race	90
Table 37	Teenaged Childbearing Rates by Mother's Age and Race, 1975	91
Table 38	Percentage of Live Births Whose Mothers Were Teenaged at Time of Birth by Race, 1975	92

Table 39	Percentage of Illegitimate Live Births to Teenaged Mothers by Mother's Education, Age, and Race, 1975	93
Table 40	Children's Death Rates by Age and Race, 1975	94
Table 41	Death Rates of Children Aged 15-19 by Cause of Death, Sex, and Race, 1975	95
Table 42	Percentage of Children Aged 1-4 and 5-9 Living in U.S. Central Cities Who Are Not Immunized against Major Preventable Diseases by Disease, Age, and Race, 1978	96
Table 43	Percentage of Children with Nutritional Intake below Established Standards by Nutrient, Age, and Race, 1971-1974	97
Table 44	Percentage of Children Who Eat Specific Food Groups Less Frequently than Once a Day by Age and Race, 1971-1974	98
Table 45	Rate of Newly Detected Active Tuberculosis Cases by Age, Sex, and Race, 1974	99
Table 46	Percentage of Children under 15 by Source of Health Care and Race, 1975	100
Table 47	Percentage of Children under 17 Who Have Not Seen a Doctor in the Last Year by Age and Race, 1977	101
Table 48	Dental Visits of Children under 17 by Race, 1976-1977	102
Table 49	Percentage of the Population under 17 Lacking Private Hospital and Surgical Insurance Coverage by Family Income and Race, 1974	103
Table 50	Rates of Admission to State and County Mental Hospitals by Type of Admission, Age, Sex, and Race, 1975	104

Table 51   Drug and Alcohol Use among Youths by Race   105

Housing   106

　Table 52   Percentage of Children Living in Inadequate Housing by Family Structure, Rental Status, and Race, Fall 1977   107

Children Without Homes   108

　Table 53   Number of Children Not Living with Relatives or in Institutions by Age, Residential Arrangement, and Race, March 1978   109

　Table 54   Persons in Institutions: Median Age and Length of Stay by Type of Institution and Race, Spring 1976   110

　Table 55   Children in Institutions by Sex and Race, 1976   111

　Table 56   Percentage of Disabled Child Beneficiaries of Supplemental Security Income by Type of Placement and Race, 1977   112

Crime and Arrests   113

　Table 57   Death Rates from Homicide by Age, Sex, and Race, 1975   114

　Table 58   Arrest Rates for Youths Aged 11-17 by Type of Offense and Race, 1975   115

　Table 59   Rates of Personal Victimization by Serious Crime for Youths Aged 12-19 by Age, Sex, and Race, 1974   116

Part I

Introduction

> You have no right to enjoy a child's share in the labors of your fathers unless your children are to be blest by your labors.
> Frederick Douglass[1]

Reggie Jackson is a millionaire. Coleman Young is mayor of Detroit. Diana Ross and Michael Jackson are superstars. Richard Hatcher is president of the Conference of Mayors. Amalyia Kearse is the first woman judge on the Second Circuit Court of Appeals. Thurgood Marshall sits on the United States Supreme Court. Patricia Harris is a member of the President's cabinet. Andrew Young is a household word. Many Black children and families are thriving and succeeding. More Black young people are attending college, becoming doctors and lawyers, going to graduate school, and moving into the middle class.

But despite these examples of success, Black children, youths, and families remain worse off than whites in every area of American life. After decades of systematic segregation and discrimination, the rising tide of opportunity that swelled during the 1960s was neither long enough nor strong enough to enable most Black children to gain the opportunities most white children take for granted. Millions of Black children were left behind when the progress begun in the 1960s leveled off or declined in the 1970s. Although the Black middle class grew, the Black poor grew at a faster rate. The median income in real dollars for Blacks actually fell, and the income gap between Blacks and whites widened by 14 percent. The relative share of admissions between 1973 and 1978

---

[1] Frederick Douglass, "The Meaning of July Fourth for the Negro," in *The Voice of Black America*, ed. Philip Foner (New York: Simon and Schuster, 1972), p. 113.

for Blacks into law, medical, and professional schools declined.[2] What happens to the children left behind? Some have abandoned hope, like those who participated in the recent Miami riots:

> They are small boys, 11, 12, 13 years old, still blushing when asked about their girlfriends... But when guns and homemade bombs explode on the streets here, they stand on the sidewalks with the older boys, hurling rocks and bottles at every passing white motorist...
>
> In the slums here, where in some neighborhoods eight of every 10 young black men are out of work, where one teeming apartment complex has been so overrun with trash and filth that everyone calls it "Germ City," they say again and again there is no hope.
>
> No hope. And, as a result now, no fear.[3]

Others are still trying to keep going, despite staggering obstacles. A 15-year-old Black youth describes the world he sees:

> ...**School and Street:** In Brooklyn you fall into one of two categories when you start growing up. The names for the categories may be different in other cities, but the categories are the same. First, there's the minority of the minority, the "ducks," or suckers. These are the

---

[2] By 1979, there was 1 Black doctor for every 728 Black persons, a 25 percent improvement since 1972, and 1 Black lawyer for every 2,295 Black persons, a 48 percent improvement in the same period. (This compares with 1 white doctor for every 484 white persons and 1 white lawyer for every 389 white persons.) But the growth has leveled off at its source, professional school admissions. Between 1973 and 1978, there was an 11 percent decline in the proportion Black of first-year medical school enrollments; the number of first-year Black medical students held just under 1,100 for the whole period. Two hundred were at predominantly Black Meharry Medical School. From 1973 to 1977, the proportion Black of first-year law students declined by 6 percent, with the number of first-year Black law students just over 1,940 in both years. U.S. Department of Labor, Bureau of Labor Statistics, *Employment and Earnings*, Vol. 27 No. 1 (January 1980), Table 23; U.S. Department of Commerce, Bureau of the Census, *Statistical Abstract of the United States: 1979* (100th edition) (Washington, DC: U.S. Government Printing Office, 1979), Table 687; National Advisory Committee on Black Higher Education and Black Colleges and Universities, *Access of Black Americans to Higher Education: How Open Is The Door?* (Washington, DC: U.S. Government Printing Office, January 1979), p. 26 and Tables 13 and 14, calculations by the Children's Defense Fund.

[3] Herbert Denton, "Riot Without Rhetoric: Small Boys in Black Miami Vent Despair on 'Crackers'," *The Washington Post* (July 30, 1980), pp. 1, 4-5. The author describes "the dismaying whispering conversation" of a group of young friends about dinner. "What became clear was that on that night, like others, there would not be food on the table in every apartment."

kids who go to school every day. They even want to go to college. Imagine that! School after high school! They don't smoke cheeb (marijuana) and they get zooted (intoxicated) after only one can of beer. They're wasting their lives waiting for a dream that won't come true.

The ducks are usually the ones getting beat up on by the majority group—the "hard rocks." If you're a real hard rock you have no worries, no cares. Getting high is as easy as breathing. You just rip off some duck. You don't bother going to school; it's not necessary. You just live with your mom until you get a job—that should be any time a job comes looking for you. Why should you bother to go look for it? Even your parents can't find work.

I guess the barrier between the ducks and the hard rocks is the barrier of despair. The ducks still have hope, while the hard rocks are frustrated. They're caught in the deadly, dead-end environment and can't see a way out. Life becomes the fast life—or incredibly boring—and death becomes the death that you see and get used to every day. They don't want to hear any more promises. They believe that's just the white man's way of keeping them under control.

Bravado: Hard rocks do what they want to do when they want to do it. When a hard rock goes to prison it builds up his reputation. He develops a bravado that's like a long, sad joke. But it's all lies and excuses. It's a hustle to keep ahead of the fact that he's going nowhere....

I guess the best way to help the hard rocks is to help the ducks. If the hard rocks see the good guy making it, maybe they will change. If they see the ducks, the ones who try, succeed, it might bring them around. The ducks are really the only ones who might be able to change the situation.

The problem with most ducks is that after years of effort they develop a negative attitude, too. If they succeed, they know they've got it made. Each one can say he did it by himself and for himself. No one helped him and he owes nobody anything, so he says, "Let the hard rocks and the junkies stay where they are"—the old every-man-for-himself routine.

What the ducks must be made to realize is that it was this same attitude that made the hard rocks so hard. They developed a sense of kill or be killed, abuse or be abused, take it or get taken.

The hard rocks want revenge. They want revenge because they don't have any hope of changing their situation. Their teachers don't offer it, their parents have lost theirs, and their grandparents died with a heartful of hope but nothing to show for it.

Maybe the only people left with hope are the only people who can make a difference—teens like me. We, the ducks, must learn to care. As a 15-year-old, I'm not sure I can handle all that. Just growing up seems hard enough.[4]

We adults must also learn to care more and help the ducks help the hard rocks. The tables in this book show why millions of Black children lack self-confidence, feel discouragement, despair, numbness, or rage as they try to grow up on islands of poverty, ill health, inadequate education, squalid streets riddled with dilapidated housing, crime, and rampant unemployment in a nation of boastful affluence.

There are no quick or easy fixes for the problems described in this book. *But many of them can be alleviated or solved.* In addition to the facts, included here is a practical set of steps for all Americans; for key policymakers; and especially for Black organizations, churches, colleges, leaders, and parents to take to remove the barriers that sap the hopes, waste the talents, and relegate millions of Black children and youths to lifelong dependency. While the goals outlined will not solve every problem Black children and their families face, or give them the same chance to succeed as white middle-class children, their accomplishment will significantly improve the quality of life for millions of Blacks and for our nation.

This book is organized into two major sections. Part I draws a

---

[4] Deairich Hunter, "Ducks Vs. Hard Rocks," in *Newsweek* (August 18, 1980), pp. 14-15. Copyright 1980 by *Newsweek*, Inc. All rights reserved. Reprinted by permission. Mr. Hunter writes a monthly column for *The Eye*, a student news magazine based in Wilmington, Delaware.

composite portrait of inequality facing Black children in America today. It is followed by 11 premises for effective advocacy to change this portrait and an action agenda of specific, practical goals for improving conditions for Black children, youths, and families now and in the foreseeable future. They are neither new nor "catchy." *But they have not been and must be done.*

Part II presents the most recent statistical data available to document the persistent disparities between Black and white children, youths, and families. The data are organized into sections on numbers of children and families, family structure, poverty, unemployment, maternal employment and child care, education, health, housing, foster care and institutionalization, and crime and arrests. Each of these sections contains a short summary of the principal facts in the tables that follow. Most of the numbers used in Part I come from the tables and sources in Part II. Exceptions are footnoted.

I am grateful to Paul Smith, CDF's director of research, who compiled the data contained in this book, to Rochelle Beck and Janet King, who edited it, and to all those who read, commented on, and endlessly typed this manuscript. I take full responsibility, however, for the judgments and conclusions expressed here. The Children's Defense Fund stands ready to work with all those who want to achieve the goals recommended in this book.

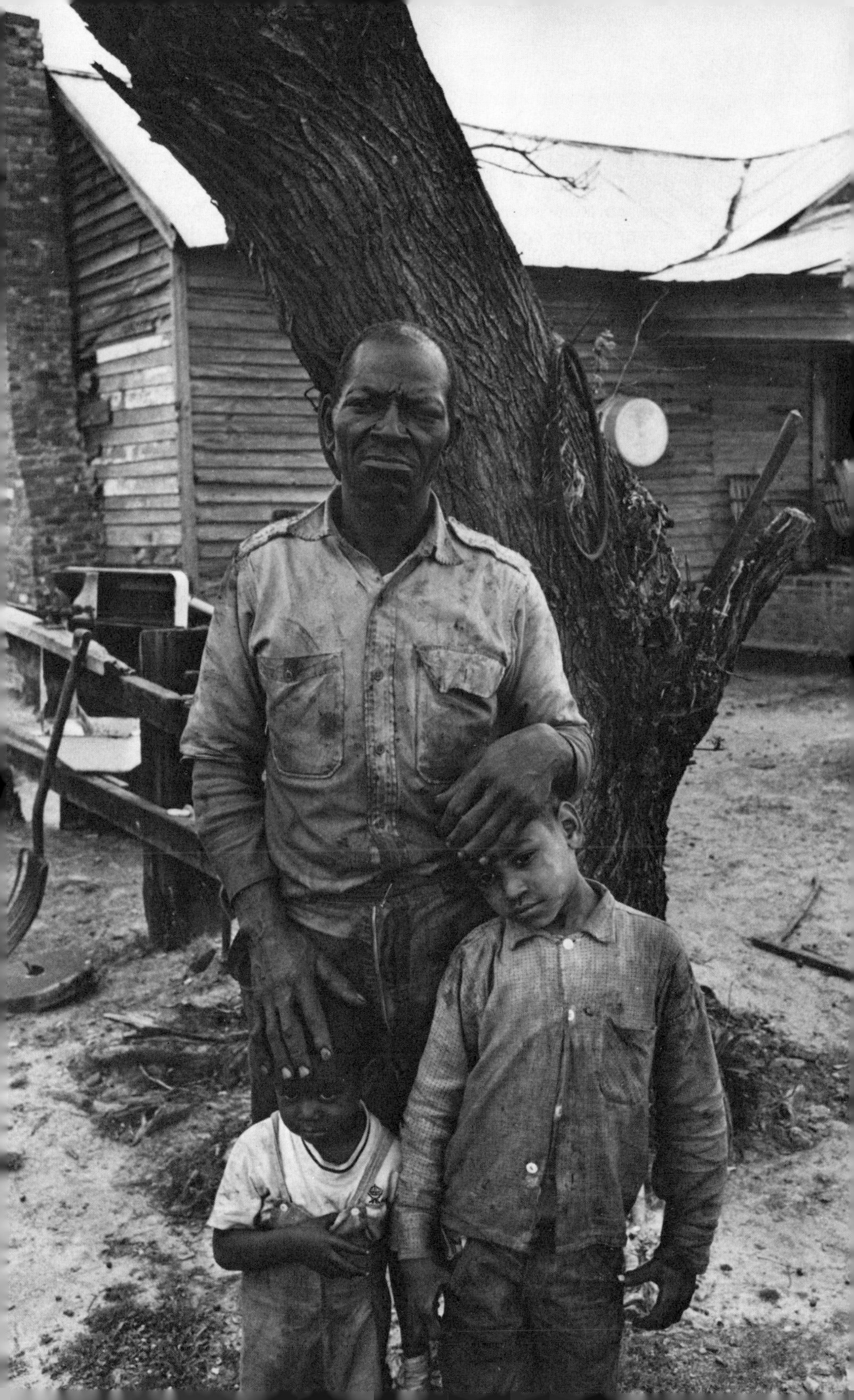

A Portrait of Inequality

A Black child still lacks a fair chance to live, learn, thrive, and contribute in America.

A Black baby is three times as likely as a white baby to have a mother who dies in childbirth and is twice as likely to be born to a mother who has had no prenatal care at all. A Black infant is twice as likely as a white infant to die during the first year of life. The Black infant mortality rate in 1978 was about the same as the white infant mortality rate in 1950.

Black teenagers die from heart and congenital defects at twice the rate of white teenagers, and Black teenaged girls die from heart disease at three times the rate of white teenaged girls. There are five times as many newly detected tuberculosis cases among Black as among white children.

Black children are more likely to be sick because they are more likely to be poor. They are twice as likely as white children to have no regular source of health care, are likely to be more seriously ill when they finally do see a doctor, and are five times as likely to have to rely on hospital emergency rooms or outpatient clinics.

A Black baby today has nearly a one in two chance of being born into poverty and faces a losing struggle to escape poverty throughout childhood. A Black child is more than two-and-one-half times as likely as a white child to live in dilapidated housing and is twice as likely to be on welfare. A Black child's mother is more likely to go out to work sooner, to work longer hours, and to make less money than a white child's mother. As a result, young Black children are far more dependent on full-time day care arrangements than white children.

A Black child's father is 70 percent more likely than a white child's father to be unemployed, and when Black fathers find work, they bring home $70 a week less than white fathers. When both parents work, they earn only half what a white family earns.

A Black child is twice as likely as a white child to live with neither parent, three times as likely to be born to a teenaged mother, seven times as likely to have parents who separate, and three times as likely to see his father die.

A Black child is three times as likely as a white child to live in a single-parent home. A Black preschool child is three times as likely to depend solely on a mother's earnings. Because the Black woman still faces discrimination as a Black and as a woman, she is the lowest paid among workers and her female-headed family is the poorest in the nation.

A Black child is twice as likely as a white child to grow up in a family whose head did not finish high school and is four times less likely than a white child to grow up in a family whose head graduated from college.

In school, a Black child faces a one in three chance of being in a racially isolated school and is twice as likely as a white child to be suspended, expelled, or given corporal punishment. A Black child is twice as likely as a white child to drop out of school, almost twice as likely to be behind grade level, three times as likely to be labeled educable mentally retarded, but only half as likely to be labeled gifted. The longer a Black child is in school, the farther behind he or she falls.

A Black youth is three times as likely as a white youth to be unemployed. A Black student who graduates from high school has a greater chance of being unemployed than a white student who dropped out of elementary school. A Black college graduate faces about the same odds of unemployment as a white high school dropout.

Between the ages of 11 and 17, a Black teenager has more than a one in ten chance of getting into trouble, is seven times as likely as a white youth to be arrested for violent crimes, and is twice as likely to be arrested for serious property crimes. A Black male teenager is five times as likely as a white male teenager to be a victim of homicide and is twice as likely to be detained in a juvenile or adult correctional facility—the conclusion of a winding, uphill struggle to beat the odds against success.

To Change the Portrait

Many Americans reading this grim portrait of inequality will ask, "Why bother? These children are losers. Let's write them off, not waste our efforts, and get on with the business of helping our own children or those who can benefit more from our attention." There are compelling reasons not to write these children off.

First, a fair start and chance in life is every American child's birthright. To continue to deny opportunity to millions of children in our midst is to erode the fundamental premises upon which our society rests. Young people unfairly treated will not respect or value these premises as adults. Their alienation and resentment is a built-in time bomb that poses a threat to us all.

Second, it is more cost effective to help rather than to neglect children. With a relatively modest investment in fairly administered and preventive measures, children can grow into assets. To the extent that their skills and talents are developed, our productivity as a nation is enhanced and our burden to provide for them, decreased. To the extent they are ignored, benignly neglected, or shunted aside, we will have to fear, support, or even imprison them. For example:

- In the ten years after measles vaccine was introduced, the cost savings were estimated to be $1.3 billion.[5]
- The total health costs for children receiving regular primary and preventive health care are roughly 40 percent less than for children who do not get such care.[6]
- In 1978, over 650,000 14- to 17-year-old students were two or more years behind grade level. If improved education had prevented their grade retention even *one* year, the nation might

---

[5] Statement of Dr. Julius B. Richmond, Assistant Secretary for Health and Surgeon General, U.S. Public Health Service, Department of Health, Education, and Welfare, September 28, 1979.

[6] See, for example, Community Health Foundation (Evanston, IL), "Cost Impact Study of the North Dakota EPSDT Program," September 1977 (processed).

have saved some $1.3 billion in education costs.[7] In addition, these students might have contributed more to society by being less likely to drop out of high school and more likely to enter the labor force and pay taxes.
- In August 1979, Aid to Families with Dependent Children (AFDC) paid an average of $1,159 per child per month for institutional care, an average of $260 per child per month for foster family care, and an average of $134 per month for children living with their families. If as few as 10 percent of the children in out-of-home care could be shifted to family settings, the savings would be well over $25 million per year.[8]

Third, hurting or neglecting some children hurts all our children. Many Americans mistakenly think it is only "other people's children"—poor, Black, Hispanic, Native American—who have problems. But the problems these children disproportionately suffer affect large numbers of middle-class and white children, too. More white than Black children are poor, on welfare, ill educated, and without adequate child care or health care. School vandalism, school violence, drug and alcohol abuse, teenaged pregnancy, and illegitimacy are major problems in all communities, striking all races and classes. Suicide rates are rising more rapidly among white 15-to 19-year-old males than among any other group in our society.[9]

It has been the historic lot of the minority community, from its greater desperation and need, to point the way to greater public awareness of and responsiveness to human needs. But it is all

---

[7] This is based on an annual per child school expenditure in school year 1978-79 of $1,993. If improved instruction eliminated one extra year of schooling for all children who lose at least one year, we would save $7.0 billion at 1978 prices ($1,993 for 3.5 million pupils). U.S. Department of Commerce, Bureau of the Census, *Current Population Reports*, Series P-20, No. 346, "School Enrollment—Social and Economic Characteristics of Students: October 1978" (Washington, DC: U.S. Government Printing Office, 1979), Table 15; U.S. Department of Education, National Center for Education Statistics, unpublished data from the Elementary and Secondary General Information System, Fall 1978, calculations by the Children's Defense Fund.
[8] These very conservative figures are based on moving 10 percent of the 13,524 AFDC children in institutions to foster care and 10 percent of the 77,959 AFDC children in foster care back to their own families. U.S. Department of Health, Education, and Welfare, Social Security Administration, *Public Assistance Statistics*, ORS Report A-2 (8/79), "Public Assistance Statistics, August 1979" (Washington, DC: Social Security Administration, March 1980), Tables 4 and 7, calculations by the Children's Defense Fund.
[9] Data showing the large number of white children affected by the problems that disproportionately hurt Black children appear in the tables throughout Part II of this book.

children and taxpayers who will benefit from health, education, welfare, and other systems that operate efficiently, effectively, and fairly.

Middle-class Black Americans who ask why they should help poor Black children after they have struggled so hard to make it themselves must pause in their climb up the slippery slope of upward mobility. W.E.B.Dubois told young Black graduates in 1907 that if they really had "at heart the good of the world, you simply cannot give your whole time and energy to the selfish seeking of your personal good. If you wish the Negro race to become honest, intelligent, and rich, you cannot make accumulation of wealth for yourself the sole object of your education and life." He counseled them to "be your brother's keeper as well as your own, or your brother will drag you and yours down to his ruin."[10]

Color and history inextricably bind the fate of all Blacks. The Ku Klux Klan does not segregate its racial hatred by class. Police do not usually check income before stopping us or our children in neighborhoods where we are still not expected or wanted. When some Black youths lash out in frustration, they burn down Black areas as well as white businesses and terrorize other Black youths and old people as well as whites. An eroding climate for social justice and backlash against affirmative action keep poor Blacks out of entry level jobs or promotions; but they also narrow the gates to graduate and professional schools for middle-class Blacks. Budget and social program cuts hurt the poor, but they also hamstring Black mayors trying to run cities. Unemployment crushes Black families struggling to survive, but it threatens the health of Black businesses and other institutions dependent on Black purchasing power and income as well.

Fourth, all Black children are our "growing edge" as a people and as a nation. Our task as adults is to nourish and protect them despite the growing national negativism about meeting social needs. Our role as adults must be like the particular kind of oak tree described by Howard Thurman, the noted Black theologian. Though its leaves turn yellow and die, they stay on the tree all winter. The wind, the storm, the snow—nothing is able to dislodge the leaves from their apparently dead branches. They hang on until spring, when a stirring deep within the heart of the tree begins and

---

[10] "St. Francis of Assisi," address delivered at the Joint Commencement Exercises of Miner Normal School, M Street High School, and Armstrong Manual Training School, Washington, DC, June 1907, in *A W.E.B. Dubois Reader*, ed. Andrew G. Paschal (New York: Collier Books, 1971), p. 300.

the expression of its life reverses itself. The dead leaves then fall off. In their places, buds begin to form—the tree's growing edge, its life force, its renewal.[11]

So it is with us and our children, who are our growing edge and renewal as a people. Black adults, like the oak, must shield, nourish, and stand up for Black children until the national climate permits them to grow and flourish as fully as white children.

While we must take the lead, the task of erasing the barriers to equal opportunity does not rest solely on the backs of the Black community. Just as the entire nation condoned slavery and segregation for decades, so the entire nation must work to reverse their effects. The President and his cabinet; the Congress; governors; mayors; corporations; private sector leaders; citizens; and Black parents, organizations, and leaders everywhere must adopt and implement a conscious, targeted, and programmatic agenda in order to bolster the self-sufficiency of the Black family and Black community and close the gaps described in this book.

But history makes plain that without strong and persistent Black leadership, the nation will ignore the needs of Black children and families. Although the premises for effective advocacy that follow are aimed primarily at the Black community and draw on Black history and experience, the principles are applicable to all those seeking to solve social problems. If Black parents, organizations, churches, and leaders are to help transform the nation's attitudes and responses toward Black children and families, we must first transform our own attitudes and understand the precepts essential to combating the inequality that destroys so many of our young.

---

[11] Howard Thurman, *The Growing Edge* (Indiana: Friends United Press, 1956), p. 177.

Eleven Premises for Effective Advocacy

1 **Become an active and effective advocate for Black and poor children.** We all must take a stronger, more systematic, and more programmatic interest in alleviating the problems that affect Black children. No one has a greater stake than we do in whether our children read, write, think, survive, and grow up healthy. If the widespread nutrition, health, child care, education, and employment needs described in this book are to be met, Black parents and leaders must constantly raise them in public, organize to challenge them, and vote for leaders who will do something about them.[12]

2 **Become well informed about the needs of Black children and families in your area and nationally.** We will not help Black children if we are uninformed. We must argue with facts as well as with emotion. We must teach as well as preach. Homework is a key to effective change. We must take the time to define specifically the problems facing children in our communities. We must then analyze and seek a range of appropriate remedies within our own families and institutions and through appropriate policy changes in other institutions. Those who care about Black children and families should hold study groups in churches and in women's, civic, and social clubs; invite speakers knowledgeable about and active on behalf of children; and find out how to achieve specific positive policies for children.[13]

3 **Don't give or accept excuses for doing nothing.** Too many of us hide behind excuses:
"Whatever I do won't make a difference anyway."

---

[12] For a step-by-step description of how parents and others can become more effective child advocates, see *It's Time to Stand Up for Your Children: A Parent's Guide to Child Advocacy* (Washington, DC: Children's Defense Fund, 1979).

[13] For sources and pointers to help you do research on the needs of children in your community, see *Where Do You Look? Whom Do You Ask? How Do You Know? Information Resources for Child Advocates* (Washington, DC: Children's Defense Fund, 1980). In addition, facts about children's needs and strategies for addressing them appear in other CDF publications and in our monthly newsletter, *CDF Reports*. For information, call our toll-free line, (800) 424-9602.

"I've already done my bit or paid my dues. Now I'm going to get mine."

"It'll just get me and my child into trouble."

These and other do-nothing excuses are an abnegation of personal responsibility for one another and for our children. We are not out of the woods because some of us have two cars, a big mortgage, and several charge accounts. Any Black person who thinks this way is courting danger and jeopardizing our children's future.

The Black community stands poised today between progress and regression. We should heed Frederick Douglass's warning about how fragile change is when he said:

> I know that from the acorn evolves the oak, but I know also that the commonest accident may destroy its potential character and defeat its natural destiny. One wave brings its treasure from the briny deep, but another sweeps it back to its primal depths. The saying that revolutions never go back must be taken with limitations.[14]

The hard-earned progress of the 1950s and 1960s is not a keepsake that can be taken for granted. Indeed, it is threatened daily. There is a growing resistance to affirmative action, programs targeted for the poor, increased government spending, and strong federal regulations. There is a defense budget that is regarded by many as a tradeoff for children's futures. And there is a national impatience that resents the fact that the effects of centuries of segregation and discrimination did not disappear quietly and cheaply in a decade or two. The revival of Ku Klux Klan activity, increasing clashes between the police and Black communities, and threatened retrenchment of Black political power through restrictive judicial interpretation of the Voting Rights Act of 1965 are all causes for concern.

The Black community must be constantly vigilant lest our rights and our children's futures are undermined by subtle and not-so-subtle means. Today's atmosphere, against the end of the Reconstruction era and the backsliding on equal opportunity during the Nixon and Ford Administrations, should be adequate warning.

---

[14] Frederick Douglass, "The Mission of the War," in *The Voice of Black America*, p. 284.

4 **Understand clearly that nobody is going to give us or our children anything.** Frederick Douglass put it bluntly: "Men may not get all they pay for in this world, but they must certainly pay for all they get."[15] Whatever we achieve for Black children and families will depend more on what we do with our votes and political power than on what those in power do on their own. We must vote strategically and intelligently and, through our example and leadership, encourage Black youths to participate in the political process.[16]

Even as we seek additional resources and laws, we must constantly monitor the enforcement of laws already on the books, help weed out those that do not work, and see how existing money can be better used to reach the children intended to be served. For example, only one-sixth of the children eligible for Medicaid get the Early and Periodic Screening, Diagnosis and Treatment (EPSDT) services to which they are entitled.[17] These children are disproportionately Black. Tens of thousands more children could receive needed health services *now* if their families knew of the program's availability and if Black organizations demanded better enforcement of that law by states and the federal government.

5 **Recognize that the ground rules for achieving change are different now than they were five or ten years ago.** The resource pie is contracting. The burden of proof and the level of competency required of groups seeking social change have increased. We cannot represent the interests of children and families effectively simply by asserting that what we want is morally right. We cannot look at children's or poor people's or civil rights programs and simply ask for more money.

We must gain greater technical proficiency in how bureaucracies work; how programs are administered; how services are delivered;

---

[15] Frederick Douglass, "If There Is No Struggle, There Is No Progress," in *The Voice of Black America*, p. 200.
[16] Only 27.7 percent of Black youths aged 18-20 are registered to vote. Black voter participation rates for this age group are 30 percent below white voter participation rates. Current efforts by a number of Black organizations to register young voters and get them out to vote must be continued and strengthened. U.S. Department of Commerce, Bureau of the Census, *Current Population Reports*, Series P-20, No. 344, "Voting and Registration in the Election of November 1978" (Washington, DC: U.S. Government Printing Office, September 1979), Table 2.
[17] U.S. Department of Health, Education, and Welfare, Health Care Financing Administration, Medicaid/Medicare Management Institute, *Data on the Medicaid Program: Eligibility/Services/Expenditures*, 1979 Edition (Revised)(Baltimore, MD: Health Care Financing Administration, 1979).

and how budget decisions are made at the federal, state, and local levels. We must be aware of and learn to influence the complicated tradeoffs that are made by those in power. Whoever controls the budget controls policy and will have a critical impact on jobs and services for Black families in the decade to come.[18]

6 **Focus attention and energies.** We should always maintain our vision and work toward longer-range goals for Black children and the Black community. But we must break down our big goals into manageable, practical pieces for action. Too much of our current effort is diluted by our failure to set priorities and stick with them until they are accomplished. Too many possible, incremental gains are overlooked while we focus on long-term agendas we cannot accomplish in the foreseeable future. We must act now to deal with our children's immediate needs for adequate nutrition, education, child care, health care, and family stability. They only grow up once. Another generation should not be sacrificed while we work toward ideal solutions. A child health bill that we can help pass now, for instance, is worth a lot more than a national health insurance program that may or may not pass in the next five years or at all.[19] We must set specific immediate, intermediate, and long-range goals and go systematically, step by step, until we achieve them.

7 **Expend energy on real issues, not symbolic ones.** We must not be bought off by appeals to vanity or status. We must avoid a treadmill of endless consultations and meetings that result in little or no action. Consultations, conferences, and commissions are not substitutes for programs and money. We must set substantive goals, think about how to achieve them, and choose the means that get us there.

There is another, more important dimension to this substance-versus-symbolism issue for the Black community. Nannie Burroughs, a leading Black churchwoman, spoke of the need for Black people to organize "inside" and to teach our children

...the internals and eternals rather than the externals. Be more concerned with putting in than getting on. We

---

[18] See a forthcoming CDF publication, *Children and the Federal Budget*, for more information on how to participate in federal budget decisions.
[19] Therefore, one of CDF's top 1980 legislative priorities is passage of the Child Health Assurance Program (CHAP, S. 1204 and H.R. 4962), even as we work toward national health insurance.

have been too bothered about the externals—clothes or money. What we need are mental and spiritual giants who are aflame with a purpose.[20]

In the 1980s, we must focus more on what is in our children's heads and hearts and less on what is on their backs and feet. Black people have always brought a special dimension to our nation because of our struggle for freedom and equality. We must not squander it by buying into the materialistic values of the culture and abandoning the commitment to serve others that our past has dictated. We have not come so far to seize so little.

8 **Persist and dig in for a long fight.** Recognize that a major agenda for Black children and families is possible and essential—but will not be achieved overnight. There are no miracles on the horizon to make the dream of equal opportunity a reality for Black children. There are no Moseses or Kings in the wings to lead us to light. We must each take the responsibility for lifting ourselves and bringing along others. Everything we have earned as a people—even that which is our own by right—has come out of long struggle. The latest civil rights movement did not start in the 1950s. It started in the 1930s with a small band of brave parents and lawyers plotting to challenge legal segregation. As in past decades, nothing is more likely to bring about change now for our children than determination and persistence.

9 **Use what you have to do what you must.** Don't hide behind lack of education or wealth as a reason for inactivity or despair. To do so is to betray a central quality of our history and key to our futures. Our attitude must be like the father on a plantation in Issaquena County, Mississippi, when his child's Head Start center did not appear to have any chance of being refunded: "...if there is no way, we'll find a way anyway."[21] And they did.

Sojourner Truth, a woman who could neither read nor write, pointed the way for us. She never gave up talking or fighting against slavery and the mistreatment of women, not even against odds far worse than those we and our children face today. Once a

---

[20] Nannie H. Burroughs, "Unload Your Uncle Toms," in *Black Women in White America: A Documentary History*, ed. Gerda Lerner (New York: Vintage Books, 1972), pp. 552-553.
[21] Polly Greenberg, *The Devil Has Slippery Shoes* (Toronto, Ontario: The Macmillan Company, 1969), p. 1.

heckler told Sojourner that he cared no more for her talk "than for a fleabite." "Maybe not," was her answer, "but the Lord willing, I'll keep you scratching."[22]

Her retort should be ours today and tomorrow to a nation that keeps turning its back on our children. Although many politicians, voters, school teachers, corporations, and unions do not really want to hear or act on the problems of our families and children, Black parents and leaders have got to make them scratch all over the nation. Every single person can be a flea and can bite. However poor, however unlearned, everybody can stand up for a child who's mistreated. Enough fleas for children can make even the biggest dogs mighty uncomfortable. If they flick some of us off and others of us keep coming back, we will begin to get our children's needs heard and attended to.

10 **Attack the right enemy. Stand united.** We remain our own worst enemies. Some Black people spend more time fighting and picking at each other than at the real opponents of Black children and families. Too many of us are forever looking over our shoulders to see who else is doing something. People who always look over their shoulders are not looking ahead. The facts in this book make plain that there is plenty for all of us to do without stepping on each other's toes. Let us pull together. It is Black children who lose from our ego-tripping and fragmentation. How can we expect other people to place our children's needs higher than their own interests if we ourselves do not? And how can we ask others to invest more time, energy, and service than we do? Our ideas will not work unless we do.

11 **Teach our children our history so that they can gain confidence, self-reliance, and courage.** I recall hearing Mary McLeod Bethune, who founded Bethune-Cookman College, talking about the need to arm ourselves with the facts of our past so that we and our children could face the future with clear eyes and sure vision. Yet there are some Black youngsters in our urban schools who have never heard of Martin Luther King, Jr. There are talented Black students in Ivy League universities who complain about how tough it is to get an education. There are Black youths who neither know who Benjamin Mays is nor what he went through to get from the town of Ninety Six,

---

[22] *Black Women in White America*, p. 524.

South Carolina, to Bates College, to become the president of Morehouse College.[23] Too many Black students in Black colleges today do not know the debt they owe John Lewis or that Andrew Young earned his way to fame by way of the jailhouse and billyclub. They have not basked in the eloquence of Frederick Douglass, Countee Cullen, or James Weldon Johnson or escaped slavery and death with Harriet Tubman. They do not know the Negro national anthem, "Lift Every Voice and Sing," that many of us Black adults learned before "The Star Spangled Banner." They have not flared up indignantly against discrimination with Sojourner Truth or laughed with Langston Hughes's "Simple" or raged with Claude McKay.[24] They are unaware of the contributions Charles Drew and Ralph Bunche made to world health and peace. Too many of our children are not anchored in the faith of a Bethune, who could envision and start a college on a dump heap and promised downpayment of $5.00 that she did not have. They do not sense or share deeply enough the sorrowful despair channeled into song and sermon that allowed our grandparents, fathers, and mothers to keep going when times were so tough. They are missing the pride, confidence, and purpose of a Nanny Burroughs, who boasted about specializing "in the wholly impossible."[25]

More critically, too many of our middle-class children do not know the dangers of taking anything for granted in America or what remains to be done to achieve justice because we adults are not sufficiently teaching them and leading the way. That is the task before us now if the portrait of inequality drawn here is to develop into a portrait of hope.

The 1980's may look complex and bleak. But not as complex and bleak as what the Tubmans, Truths, Douglasses, Bethunes, Duboises, Everses, Parkses, and Kings faced when they began to stand up for our children and for the justice to which the Black community is entitled. That is what each of us must do now: find the ways to help those of our Black—and white and brown and red—children still left behind and to guide the nation away from the moral shame, the ongoing toll of dependency, lost talent, foregone productivity, and unrealized promise that ignoring our children brings.

---

[23] See Benjamin E. Mays, *Born to Rebel: An Autobiography* (New York: Scribner, 1971).
[24] See, for example, Langston Hughes, *Simple's Uncle Sam* (New York: Hill and Whang, 1965).
[25] *Black Women in White America*, p. 132.

An Action Agenda for Black Children

This agenda is by no means all-inclusive. It focuses on specific goals to help Black children that are critically important and that can be accomplished immediately or in the near future. It calls not only for new legislation and more resources, but also for better enforcement of laws and more efficient administration of programs already on the books. It calls for improving some programs, like the Early and Periodic Screening, Diagnosis and Treatment (EPSDT) program, that are not working well. It calls for expanding others, like Head Start, that are successful. It also calls for the enforcement of new laws—like the Adoption Assistance and Child Welfare Act of 1980, which holds promise of getting Black and other children out of costly, long-term, and discontinuous foster and institutional care. In sum, we must analyze what we have, eliminate practices and programs that do not work, build on those that do, and improve or redirect those that could be made to work better.

In looking at specific problems of and programs for children, we do not ignore the overarching importance of adequate jobs and income to Black family stability and to Black children's well-being. We will continue to lend our support to civil rights, labor, and other proponents addressing these important issues.[26] But jobs and income alone are not enough to meet children's needs. We must, in addition, find specific remedies to alleviate the education, health,

---

[26] For discussion of the effects of structural unemployment and inflation on children and families, see Kenneth Keniston and the Carnegie Council on Children, *All Our Children: The American Family Under Pressure* (New York: Harcourt Brace Jovanovich, 1977). For a series of recommendations pertaining to jobs, inflation, and economic policy, see *The National Black Agenda for the 80's: Richmond Conference Recommendations* (Washington, DC: Joint Center for Political Studies, 1980).

child welfare, child care, and housing problems daily facing millions of Black children and families. Equally important, we must change the negative attitudes and expectations that so many who teach and come into contact with Black children hold and transmit to them.

No one institution—the family, Black churches, corporations, the government—has all of the power and responsibility to meet all the needs of Black children and families. To blame or place responsibility on government or business alone would be as much a mistake as blaming parents or communities for all the problems their children face in schools, health clinics, and a range of other institutions over which they can exercise little or no control.[27] Rather, we call for the primacy of Black parents in making decisions affecting their children. They can and must exercise responsibility for their children. But public and private officials and institutions must be more sensitive to Black children and families. They must ensure that their policies and practices are fairly administered and implemented and help rather than hurt, strengthen rather than undercut, parental roles and children's well-being.

Included in this agenda are two kinds of activities: those that can be undertaken by local organizations (often using existing resources) and those that require changing the policies and practices of other institutions. Both are critically important.

Do not be overwhelmed by all that needs to be done. Take one issue or set of problems that are most pressing in your community or that most concerns your church or organization. Make a plan and begin to learn who can help you. Reach out to friends, neighbors, and local groups for support. Call CDF for assistance. Use the services we provide that are listed in the Preface.

---

[27] See, for example, *All Our Children* and *Toward a National Policy for Children and Families* (Washington, DC: National Academy of Sciences, 1976).

CHILD HEALTH

The Problem

Infant mortality. Each year, 1 out of 41 nonwhite infants (compared with 1 out of 83 white infants) dies.

Poor immunization rates. Thousands of Black children are not fully immunized against measles, polio, and other childhood diseases that we know how to prevent and that often lead to more serious illnesses or death.

Lack of prenatal services. Millions of women have no form of coverage for prenatal care. Seven out of 10 mothers under age 15 get no prenatal care in the first three months of pregnancy. One-fifth get no prenatal care at all. They are disproportionately Black. More than 1 out of 11 Black mothers receives no prenatal care until the final three months of pregnancy. There is a high correlation between lack of prenatal care and low birth weights and infant mortality and illness.

Lack of access to doctors and dentists. One out of 7 American children (or 9 million) has no regular source of primary health care—no place to go for a checkup or for treatment of routine illnesses; 1 out of 3 children under age 17 (or over 18 million) has never seen a dentist. These children are disproportionately Black. Doctors continue to leave Black ghettoes, hospitals are closed in Black neighborhoods in the name of cost containment, and preventive health care in community settings is denied or cut back.

Children having children. Some 600,000 babies are born annually to teenaged mothers; they are disproportionately Black. Their mothers often lack adequate counseling, nutrition, education, and parenting skills as well as health care.

Racial discrimination. Millions of Black children and families are victims of subtle and not-so-subtle discrimination by health officials; health professionals; and state agencies responsible for administering federal, state, and local health programs. In many states with large Black Medicaid populations, private doctors refuse to serve Medicaid patients, and state Medicaid agencies fail to reimburse community-based clinics for treating Medicaid patients.

Poor nutrition. Black children suffer from low hemoglobin levels and other indicators of malnutrition at twice the rate of white children.

Inadequate mental health care. Black children are often denied appropriate mental health services. They are less likely than white children to have had outpatient treatment prior to psychiatric hospitalization and are more than twice as likely to be admitted to inpatient psychiatric units. All too many Black children, when brought to the attention of mental health clinics, are likely to receive only diagnosis, not treatment.

Tasks for Black Communities

- Conduct education and outreach campaigns to encourage all pregnant women to get prenatal care for themselves and postnatal care for their babies. Make sure that Head Start centers, child care centers, and Black churches, as well as public agencies, provide information about the health services available in the community and their importance.
- Provide recreational and support services like counseling, discussion groups, and family planning services for teenagers to cut down on the number of unwanted teenaged pregnancies.
- Offer courses and support groups in churches and community facilities so parents can get information and advice about child health and nutrition.
- Encourage church and community hotlines and programs to visit families to see whether their children are getting needed health and social services. Let families know there are people and groups to call upon when they need help.

Goals for Improving Public Policies

Immediate

- Continue to work for more effective implementation of the nation's largest preventive health program for poor children, the Early and Periodic Screening, Diagnosis and Treatment

(EPSDT) program.[28] Advocates should ensure that families eligible for EPSDT services know about the program and can take full advantage of the benefits to which their children are entitled.
- Work for enactment and implementation of the Child Health Assurance Program (CHAP), which will improve and expand the EPSDT program. CHAP will expand Medicaid eligibility, encourage effective outreach programs for eligible families, increase the range of health services covered, develop better means for ensuring that the services get to needy children, encourage participation by qualified providers (including qualified Head Start and Title XX-funded child care centers), and strengthen the states' capacities to provide health services to needy children.
- Urge the new Department of Health and Human Services (HHS, formery HEW) to develop and enforce policies and compliance procedures under Title VI of the Civil Rights Act of 1964 to eliminate racial discrimination by health care providers and state agencies that administer health programs. Ask HHS's Office for Civil Rights to place particular emphasis on Medicaid and the Title V Maternal and Child Health Program.
- Encourage HHS and the Department of Agriculture to improve and monitor existing federal programs that finance or provide child health and child nutrition services: EPSDT; the Title V Maternal and Child Health and Crippled Children's programs; the Special Supplemental Food Program for Women, Infants, and Children (WIC); and the Child Care Food, School Lunch, and Food Stamp programs. HHS should place special emphasis on developing uniform eligibility determination procedures in order to minimize the number of children who get lost in the paper shuffle among programs.

Long-range

- Work for legislation to expand and improve support for community-based primary health care programs that have good track records for serving the Black community and delivering quality health care cost effectively.

---

[28] For details on how this program works, see *EPSDT: Does It Spell Health Care For Poor Children?* (Washington, DC: Children's Defense Fund, 1977). For specific strategies to improve the program at the local level, or for a status report on the Child Health Assurance Program (CHAP), call or write CDF.

- Work to ensure adequate mental health services for children and their families through increased, targeted funds for family support programs and other mental health services and for the training of more mental health providers.
- Work for enactment of a sound, comprehensive national health program.

CHILD CARE

The Problem

There are not enough child care services available for families who want and need them at prices they can afford. Almost 1 out of every 2 Black preschool children lives in a single-parent family. A higher proportion of Black than white mothers works full time, and they go back to work sooner after having their babies than do white mothers. A disproportionate number of children who need child care—children of working and single parents; children born to teenaged parents; children born into poverty; children at risk of abuse, neglect, or institutionalization; and children with special needs who could benefit from preschool services—are Black.

Yet Project Head Start (42 percent of whose population is Black) serves only about 20 percent of all eligible children.[29] Federal day care standards (for children primarily in Title XX-funded child care, a disproportionate number of whom are Black) have not been implemented.[30] Funds for Title XX child care services and for training child care providers have not kept pace with inflation. The child care tax credit helps middle-class families more than it does the poor: in 1978, 77 percent of tax credit benefits went to families earning more than $15,000.[31] Programs that mandate child care to enable women to participate in job training, such as the Vocational Education Amendments, have not been enforced. Several states have pressured working poor families to use AFDC Income Disregard to pay for child care instead of offering a range of child care options, including Title XX-funded programs. Money available for child care to poor and Black families from AFDC In-

---

[29] U.S. Department of Health, Education, and Welfare, Administration for Children, Youth, and Families, "Head Start Performance Indicators, Summary of Results, Fall, 1978 Program Information Report," October 1979 (processed), p. 51.
[30] Revised federal day care regulations were issued on March 19, 1980 and govern federally funded child care primarily under Titles IV-B and XX of the Social Security Act. See 45 CFR Part 71, *HEW Day Care Regulations.*
[31] U.S. Department of the Treasury, Internal Revenue Service, *Statistics of Income—1978, Individual Income Tax Returns, Preliminary Report* (Washington, DC: U.S. Government Printing Office, 1980), Table 9, calculations by the Children's Defense Fund.

come Disregard is often too little to pay for decent quality child care.[32]

Tasks for Black Communities

- Investigate what services (e.g., infant care, afterschool care, or child care during school vacations) are most needed and wanted by Black families and help set priorities for their development in your community.
- Organize to help expand the supply of family, infant, preschool, and afterschool child care in your community.[33] Consider opening up church facilities for the operation of child care programs. Work to ensure that Black communities receive their fair share of federal, state, and local public funds for child care. Explore private, corporate, and other sources of support for child care, including the United Way.
- Establish child care information, referral, and outreach programs to help parents find good child care placements. Churches and community groups can also help link families to other needed health and social services.
- Help to upgrade the quality of care provided to Black children and provide models for how parent involvement, nutrition, and other important services can be delivered through child care programs.
- Establish or expand training and technical assistance programs for child care providers through Black colleges and community organizations.
- Urge Black colleges to develop curricula and professional development programs to train child care administrators, providers, and professionals to work with Black children with special needs. Black colleges should also be urged to strengthen research and policy analysis on the needs of Black children and Black families.
- Educate the public, the press, and policymakers about the unmet need for child care. Give them examples of how much preventive

---

[32] Under AFDC Income Disregard, working parents on AFDC can "disregard" some or all of their child care expenses (how much varies widely from state to state) when the state welfare agency determines the family's AFDC benefits. Although families are eventually reimbursed in the form of increased AFDC payments, they still must have the money initially to pay for child care. Often their incomes are so limited that they can afford only poor quality care.

[33] For more information on child care policies and an agenda for the 1980s, see a forthcoming CDF book, *Who Needs Child Care? Policy Options for the '80s.*

child care programs such as Head Start have meant to Black families.

Goals for Improving Public Policies

Immediate

- Work for increases in Head Start appropriations each year to serve greater numbers of eligible children and communities. Work for increased funds for Title XX services and training and urge Congress to protect and expand the current $200 million, 100 percent federal set-aside for child care. Let the White House, the Secretary of Health and Human Services (HHS), and your congressional representatives know of your strong interest in these programs and desire for their support.
- Support the implementation and enforcement of the federal day care regulations, including training and technical assistance to help child care providers improve their programs to serve children.

Long-range

- Work for the expansion and funding of a range of publicly and privately funded child care services—including family day care homes and centers—for all families who want and need them.

EDUCATION

The Problem

Over 1 million school-aged children are not enrolled in school. They are disproportionately Black. Many are not out of school by choice but because they have been excluded. A large proportion of children expelled, repeatedly suspended, or otherwise excluded from school are "different" by virtue of race; income; physical, mental, or emotional handicap; pregnancy; marriage; or age. One out of 13 Black children was suspended from school during 1977-78, compared with 1 out of 28 white children. Frequent suspensions often cause Black children to drop out of school. There is 1 Black dropout for every 2 Black high school graduates.

Many children are not learning in school. Thousands of Black youths are unable to read, write, or compute well enough to get or keep a job. Large numbers of Black children are misclassified as mentally retarded and put in inappropriately segregated classes. Black children are placed in classes for the educable mentally retarded at three times the rate of white children. Many other children who are handicapped are not receiving the special education services they need.[34]

Tasks for Black Communities

- Try to keep children in school. Visit schools in your community. Talk to teachers, principals, and administrators and generally take an active interest in how Black children are disciplined and what the schools are teaching—or failing to teach. Become active in parent or parent/teacher groups and learn about your rights, your children's rights, and the services to which they are entitled. Do not be afraid to speak up for children, to question school decisions that may be harmful or contrary to children's

---

[34] For detailed discussion of the problems of school exclusion and misclassification, see *Children Out of School in America* (Cambridge, MA: Children's Defense Fund, 1974) and *School Suspensions: Are They Helping Children?* (Cambridge, MA: Children's Defense Fund, 1975). Also see CDF's forthcoming publication, *Misclassification: The Resegregation of Black Children in Public Schools*.

best interests, or to insist that schools discipline children fairly and try disciplinary alternatives prior to exclusion.
- Seek or sponsor tutorials and other support programs to help your child or other parents help children to develop stronger study habits. Encourage young people in churches and in the community to feel the value of education. Honor those who complete high school; support them with scholarships and encourage them to go on to college or other training.
- Encourage a lifelong interest in learning by sponsoring discussion groups, literacy programs, and continuing education for adults in the Black community. Professionals and parents alike should constantly upgrade our knowledge and skills. Teaching our children effectively means constantly teaching ourselves.
- If your child is eligible for services under Title I of the Elementary and Secondary Education Act (ESEA) or has special needs, take advantage of the participation provisions of the ESEA and the Education for All Handicapped Children Act (P.L. 94-142).
- Pay particular attention to the education needs of teenaged mothers, who frequently are school dropouts yet are responsible for raising another generation of our young.[35] Encourage them to return to school and help them find the child care that will make it possible.
- Play an active part in setting the criteria and selecting principals to ensure that the schools in your community have leaders who are receptive and willing to work with parents and who have high expectations for Black children.

Goals for Improving Public Policies

Immediate

- Challenge school exclusionary policies and practices that deprive children of an education. These include poor enforcement of the right to education for handicapped children, unnecessary suspension and expulsion, exclusion of pregnant girls, and school fees for necessary textbooks and courses which many

---

[35] Among 18- to 21-year-old high school dropouts in 1979, over 40 percent of the Black females gave pregnancy as their reason for dropping out, while less than 15 percent of the white females did so. Pregnancy and marriage combined accounted for almost half of all Black female dropouts but less than one-third of white female dropouts. U.S. Department of Education, National Center for Education Statistics, unpublished data from the 1979 U.S. Department of Labor's National Longitudinal Survey of Labor Force Behavior Youth Survey.

poor families cannot afford. Prod the new federal Department of Education immediately to develop adequate compliance procedures in the area of school discipline and to determine the extent to which racial discrimination plays a role in the disproportionate suspension and expulsion of Black children from schools. Ask your local school officials about the reasons for suspension and the suspension rates for Black and white children. Work with them to change unfair, discriminatory disciplinary policies and procedures and to develop in-school alternatives.
- Press the Department of Education and your state and local education officials to enforce Title I of ESEA, the principal federal education program designed to help disadvantaged children. Oppose attempts to dilute the focus of the program on the neediest children by turning it into a general aid or block grant program. Encourage the Department of Education to place particular emphasis on:
  - strengthening existing parental and community participation requirements and opportunities;
  - maintaining targeted funding for underserved children within schools;
  - ensuring comparable district expenditures for rich and poor children and preventing states from using federal funds as a substitute for state funds; and
  - expanding resources to meet the needs of all children requiring special education services.
- Press the Department of Education and your state and local education agencies to enforce adequately the Education for All Handicapped Children Act, which requires school districts to provide necessary and appropriate services to all handicapped children. Participate in the local planning process required under this law and encourage parents of handicapped children to participate in the development of their children's individualized education programs (IEPs). The Department of Education must develop policies and compliance procedures to prevent the inappropriate placement of large numbers of Black children in special education classes.

Long-range
- Work to ensure that every American child receives a public education suited to his or her individual needs and free from discrimination based on race, class, sex, language, or handicap.

Keep vigilant to combat crippling amendments to existing federal civil rights laws and to guard against attempts to eliminate or avoid gathering and disseminating data generated by the Office for Civil Rights Elementary and Secondary School Civil Rights Survey.[36]

---

[36] This survey is the only source of national data on school enrollment and on the status of minority, female, non-English-speaking, and handicapped children within schools. Without such data, we cannot monitor how well or how fairly these groups of children are being treated in schools throughout the country. See *The Elementary and Secondary School Civil Rights Survey: An Analysis* (Washington, DC: Children's Defense Fund, 1977).

YOUTH UNEMPLOYMENT

The Problem

Millions of Black young people face a future without hope because they cannot find work. Black teenagers are unemployed at rates nearly three times as high as the rates for white teenagers. In many inner city areas, the workless rates for young people exceed 60 percent.

Racial discrimination is a significant cause of Black youth unemployment. Sheer lack of jobs for youths is another: half the unemployed in this country are under 25. A third is the lack of job skills among Black youths. Black youths drop out of high school at nearly twice the rate white youths do, and in many of our largest cities, 1 Black youth drops out for each 1 who graduates. All too many inner city schools fail to bridge the gap between education and employment. So many inner city youths—even those who stay in school—know very little about how to look for a job or what an employer expects on the job. Many employers fail to make substantial efforts to recruit and hire inner city youths, and publicly funded vocational education and employment services seldom reach into the inner city.

Tasks for Black Communities

Immediate

- Find out how the Comprehensive Employment and Training Act (CETA) and other federal job and training dollars are being spent in your community. Is the Black community getting a fair share? Are Black community-based organizations participating in running programs for Black youths? Are the training programs focusing on careers where jobs actually exist and helping youths who are far behind in their reading and other basic skills? Are young people who have criminal records and teenaged young women who have children eligible for job training?
- Find out what private employers have been willing to do to alleviate unemployment of Black youths. Do banks hire young people from the inner city, or do they recruit only in the

suburbs? Who gets into the construction unions? Do the private employers in your area know they can qualify for a tax credit if they hire CETA-eligible youths?
- Find out what happens to federal vocational education funds that come into your community. Do the funds reach inner city schools? Are the vocational education programs helping youths prepare for good jobs, or is the training obsolete for today's job market? Find out who is on the advisory boards of the vocational schools in your community and attend their open meetings. Do the boards discuss employers' needs when planning curricula? Are Black youths being shoved into dead-end jobs? Learn about what your local and state employment services are doing to help Black youths. Find out who is on the Prime Sponsor Planning Council, the Private Industry Council, and the Youth Advisory Council required under federal CETA. Is the Black community adequately represented on these bodies?
- Find out what your schools are doing to ease the transition from school to work. Do they run joint programs with CETA prime sponsors for students who need part-time or summer jobs? Do they have cooperative or distributive education programs where students spend part of the school day working in supervised jobs for private employers? Do your local schools make sure that their students have the basic skills they need to get and hold a job? Do they prepare young people to know how the labor market works, what the options are, how to fill out a job application, how to behave during an interview, how to dress for work, and how to respond to supervision? Do the schools have placement offices to help young people get useful work experience while still in school? Do the schools participate in the Federal Career Education Incentive Program, which teaches young people about various careers and occupations and how to train for them?
- Work to improve the relationships between schools and community-based organizations that operate successful alternative education programs for Black youths. Help by carefully monitoring the quality and scope of school programs (including those paid for by CETA or vocational education dollars). Community-based organizations often provide the critical support system many Black youths need to finish school, learn about careers, and find jobs.

Long-range

- Put pressure on state education agencies to build new vocational education facilities in inner cities to give high-risk youths access to quality vocational training related to employment opportunities. In the interim, encourage the expansion of any successful vocational training programs available to inner city young people.

Goals for Improving Public Policies

Immediate

- Inform the Department of Labor and the Department of Education when you believe their money is not being well spent. Encourage these departments to take steps to ensure that funds are targeted at the youths most in need and that programs funded show substantial potential for success.
- Work for the enactment of legislation to create and fund jobs for youths. Support the bills before Congress to reauthorize and expand the CETA youth jobs programs and to add new authority and funds in both the Department of Education and the Department of Labor to improve basic skills instruction in junior and senior high schools and provide expanded work and training opportunities for young people who have dropped out of school.
- Monitor the reauthorization of the Vocational Education Act in 1981 to insure that funds are targeted at youths at high risk of unemployment. Press for a revamping of the Vocational Education Act (and its administrative agency) to insure that federal funds finance only quality programs that lead to gainful employment for youths on a nondiscriminatory basis.

CHILDREN WITHOUT HOMES

The Problem

Unnecessary removal of children from their families. Black children are disproportionately represented among the more than 500,000 children growing up in foster homes, group homes, and institutions.[37] Some of these children have been involved with the juvenile court; others have special needs stemming from physical, mental, or emotional handicaps; others have parents who have voluntarily placed their children in out-of-home care because pressures to cope were too great; still others have been abused or neglected by their parents. All too many of these children should never have been removed from their families and could have remained if their parents had been provided preventive support services like child care, homemaker services, counseling, or alternative housing. Frequently, too, public systems fail to recognize or take advantage of the informal support services available in the Black community to help families stay together—such as nearby relatives willing to care for a child or local churches willing to provide counseling or housing assistance.

Overly restrictive and inappropriate facilities. Whether they are the responsibility of the child welfare system, the juvenile justice system, or the mental health and mental retardation systems, children without homes frequently end up in settings that are inappropriate and often overly restrictive. They may be placed in institutions at great distances from their families and home communities. Other examples include runaway children placed in adult jails or children with special needs placed in institutions with no appropriate education or treatment programs.[38]

Unnecessary limbo for children. Many children, once removed from their families, remain in limbo—neither returned to their families nor provided new permanent families through adoption.

---

[37] For more information about these children, see *Children Without Homes* (Washington, DC: Children's Defense Fund, 1978).
[38] See, for instance, *Children in Adult Jails* (Washington, DC: Children's Defense Fund, 1976).

Black children, like other minority children, are especially vulnerable to public neglect by our child caring systems. Few services, if any, are provided to the children, once placed, or to their families. They are often subjected to more than one placement. And not infrequently, child welfare officials will write off Black children, especially older children, as "unadoptable." Outreach to prospective adoptive families is extremely limited.

Tasks for Black Communities

- Encourage the establishment of outreach projects, information and referral services, parent education courses, telephone hotlines, and support networks for parents who cannot cope or who are unaware of services available to them. Explore possible federal, state, county, corporate, and United Way funding for the establishment of child care centers and other services to help alleviate some of the problems that cause children to be removed from their families.
- Monitor policies and practices that affect children placed or at risk of being placed out of their homes. Ask your local child welfare department what its policies are for removing children and what attempts are made to help parents *before* children are removed. Once a child is removed, find out whether parent-child contact is encouraged and what efforts are made to return a child home as soon as possible or to find suitable adoptive families for children who cannot be returned home. Find out the number of children in out-of-home care; where they are placed; and the average length of time Black children—and other children—spend in foster homes, group homes, or institutions.
- Visit institutions that care for children. Look at the quality of care they are provided. Find out whether children are in local jails. If you suspect that children are being abused, complain to the U.S. Department of Justice. A newly enacted law, P.L. 96-247, authorizes the Justice Department to sue on behalf of children and others in state-supported facilities whose constitutional rights are being violated. Send a copy of your complaint to CDF.
- Hold discussion groups and plan strategies for reducing the incidence of out-of-home placements among Black children. Organize support groups for natural parents, foster parents, adoptive parents, and others interested in improving child welfare practices.

Goals for Improving Public Policies
Immediate

- Work for immediate implementation of the Adoption Assistance and Child Welfare Act of 1980 (P.L. 96-272), a newly enacted law that provides long overdue reforms in the child welfare system. The law redirects current federal fiscal incentives to encourage state and local officials to reduce the number of children in out-of-home care and to provide more cost-effective services to prevent placements, reunite children with their families, or provide children with appropriate adoptive families.
- Press the Department of Health and Human Services (HHS) and your state agencies to ensure that children in foster care are fully benefiting from services for which they are eligible under the Medicaid and Supplemental Security Income (SSI) programs. Similarly, urge the Department of Education to ensure that children in foster homes, group homes, and institutions are receiving their entitlements and services under the Education for All Handicapped Children Act (P.L. 94-142). Special attention should be given to the establishment by states of surrogate parent programs for children in foster care as provided for under P.L. 94-142.
- Urge HHS's Office for Civil Rights to develop nondiscrimination policies and compliance procedures under Title VI of the Civil Rights Act of 1964 and Section 504 of the Rehabilitation Act of 1973 to protect Black children placed (or at risk of being placed) out of their own homes. Current child welfare civil rights policies—like health-related civil rights policies—are skeletal at best.

Long-range

- Work for legislation that would give state and local officials further financial incentives to provide family support services and community programs as alternatives to the inappropriate institutionalization of children. Ensure appropriate services for children when they return to their communities to prevent unnecessary future institutionalization.
- Work for legislation and administrative efforts that would encourage development of a differentiated juvenile justice system that meets the needs of and protects the community from the minority of juvenile offenders who threaten its safety and serves

all others with a full range of services in the least restrictive settings appropriate to their needs.
- Work for legislation that increases the range of available medical, mental health, and social services to meet the special needs of children involved with the child welfare, juvenile justice, and mental health systems.

HOUSING DISCRIMINATION AGAINST FAMILIES WITH CHILDREN

The Problem

According to a report from the U.S. Department of Housing and Urban Development (HUD), 26 percent of all rental units ban families with children. Other restrictions based on the number, sex, or age of children apply to about 55 percent of rental units with two or more bedrooms in buildings that do accept children. The result of all these restrictions is that 47 percent of all two-bedroom rental units exclude families as a result of "no children" policies.[39]

In large cities with disproportionate numbers of Black families, the situation is worse. In Los Angeles, 70 percent of all advertised rental housing excluded or restricted children. In Dallas, 52 percent of existing apartment buildings were for adults only. In Atlanta, almost 75 percent of all new construction was restricted to adults.[40]

Housing discrimination against families with children is often a smokescreen for sex and racial discrimination. Although exclusionary practices hurt all poor families with children, those headed by women and minorities suffer especially. Black families are larger than white families and, with more children and lower incomes, find it hard to find adequate housing. Several local studies show that "no children" policies are more prevalent in "white" areas of cities than in areas with large minority populations. Thus, "no children" policies tend to perpetuate, among other things, segregated school systems. The widespread association of public housing with Black children and their families has often been cited

---

[39] University of Michigan, Survey Research Center, *Measuring Restrictive Practices Against Children in Rental Housing: A National Perspective* (Washington, DC: U.S. Department of Housing and Urban Development, 1980).

[40] U.S. Department of Housing and Urban Development, unpublished contractor reports: J G & Associates, "A Comparison of Vacancies and Rents on the Basis of Apartment Policies Regarding the Acceptance of Children," May 1979; Reid, Keating and Long, "Patterns of Discrimination Against Children in Rental Housing in the Metro-Atlanta Area," January 1979; The Fair Housing Project, "The Extent and Effects of Discrimination Against Children in Rental Housing: A Study of Five California Cities," December 1979.

as the reason for community opposition to low-income multi-family housing.

Tasks for Black Communities

- Conduct a survey to determine the extent of housing discrimination against families with children in your community. If the survey reveals specific acts of discrimination, complain to HUD. Send CDF a copy of your complaints.
- Sponsor forums to inform the community, and particularly political leaders, about the housing needs of families and children.
- Press local officials to develop Housing Assistance Plans (required under the Community Development Block Grant program) that accurately reflect the needs of low- and moderate-income families and to allocate a fair proportion of Community Development funds for the neighborhoods where these families live.
- Seek passage and enforcement of local ordinances and state statutes outlawing discrimination against families with children.[41]

Goals for Improving Public Policies

- Press HUD to produce uniform, usable data on children and housing by race. HUD must be encouraged to immediately analyze and disseminate information it collects through the Annual Housing Survey.
- Work for the immediate enactment and implementation of H.R. 5200, a bill designed to strengthen the Federal Fair Housing Law of 1968. The bill sets up an enforcement system that would enable HUD (or a state agency designated by HUD) to consider complaints speedily and where discrimination is found, order it stopped.
- Work to increase federal support for housing units for middle- and low-income families with children.
- Join with CDF's national network to combat the widespread problem of discrimination against families with children. Massive public education and challenge is needed to make this issue more visible and bring about reforms.

---

[41] A number of local groups and national organizations have begun to address this problem. See "Network Close-up," *CDF Reports*, Vol. 2, No. 1 (March, 1980). p. 5.

FAMILY SUPPORT AND SERVICES

The Problem

Poverty is the most persistent and pervasive problem affecting Black children in America. Both the absolute and the relative gaps in income for white and Black families are growing. While in 1977 1 out of every 50 Black families rose to an income of over $25,000, 1 out of every 40 Black families dropped to an income of less than $5,000. Overall, the real median income of Blacks actually fell since 1969. The income gap between Blacks and whites widened by more than 14 percent. In 1977, 1 white family in 4, compared with 1 Black family in 11, had an income over $25,000; 1 white family in 13 had an income under $5,000, compared with 1 Black family in 4. In sum, the proportion of the white poor population fell, while the proportion of the Black poor population grew. No conceivable projection of the trends of the 1970s could ever lead to equality of income in our or in our children's lifetimes.

Children are the poorest age group in society. They constitute two-thirds of all Aid to Families with Dependent Children (AFDC) recipients.[42] Two out of every 5 Black children are on AFDC in any one year. The national average AFDC payment (typically for a mother and two children) is an intolerably low $241.35 per month, and states such as Mississippi pay as little as $87.65 per month.[43] Nationally, this amounts to $83.22 a month, $19.21 a week, and $2.74 a day per person. In Mississippi, this adds up to $28.27 a month, $6.52 per week, and $.93 a day per person. Some states still maintain welfare policies that require an unemployed father to leave home as a condition of support to his family.

Jobs for all parents who want to work must be a national priori-

---

[42] AFDC (42 U.S.C.A., sec. 601 et seq. (1974)) is a partially federally funded income maintenance program for families with children. The eligibility standards and payment levels are set by individual states.

[43] These are monthly payments per family averaging 2.9 persons nationally and 3.1 persons in Mississippi, as of September 1979. U.S. Department of Health and Human Services, Social Security Administration, *Public Assistance Statistics*, ORS Report A-2 (9/79), "Public Assistance Statistics: September 1979" (Washington, DC: Social Security Administration, May 1980), Table 4.

ty. But jobs and welfare reform are not enough. Services to aid the transition out of dependency and into self-sufficiency must be adequate. Title XX of the Social Security Act is designed to provide these by funding supportive social services for low-income families. But funding has been inadequate, and the federal government has only limited means for monitoring the quality and availability of Title XX services.

Tasks for Black Communities

- Monitor the practices of your welfare department. Work to change those that are not helping families stay together or are contributing to family breakup.
- Start a public education campaign to dispel some of the myths about welfare and to inform the community that the majority of Americans who depend on AFDC are children.[44]
- Work for state legislative action to raise the level of income and benefits for families and children on AFDC.
- Gather information about and monitor the use of Title XX funds in your state and community. Try to see how much of it helps families and children. Join in the Title XX planning process. Explore applying for local United Way and corporate funds to expand the family support services available to the Black community.

Goals for Improving Public Policies

Immediate

- Urge your state officials to mandate the now-optional AFDC Unemployed Parent program so that poor families will not be penalized for having two parents living at home.
- Work for increases in the funding ceiling for Title XX to match inflation and ensure continuation of necessary child and family services at least at their current levels. Also work to maintain and increase the day care earmark within Title XX.

Long-range

- Work for enforcement of legislation to guarantee all families with a member able to work access to steady, long-term employment opportunities and all those without a member able to work

---

[44] For more information about children and their families on AFDC, see *For the Welfare of Children* (Washington, DC: Children's Defense Fund, 1978).

a uniform minimum benefit level high enough to enable children to grow into productive members of society.
- Work for legislation to ensure adequate income for children through the establishment of a national AFDC benefit floor of at least 75 percent of the poverty level.
- Press the federal government to strengthen Title XX and other social service programs through measures that would hold states more accountable for their choice of services and providers.

Part II

Numbers of Black and White Children and Families

In 1979, there were 62,380,000 children under 18 living in 30,371,000 American families;[45] 14.9 percent of the children and 12.1 percent of the families were Black; 82.8 percent of the children and 85.8 percent of the families were white.[46]

---

[45] Throughout Part II, unless otherwise indicated, "children" refers to persons under 18.

[46] Throughout Part II, we present figures for Blacks, whites, and the total population except where footnotes indicate that the source has forced some other choice, "nonwhites." In the usual cases, the "total" column will include persons of other than white or Black not shown separately.

Table 1

Number of Children in the United States by Age and Race, March 1979[a]

Age	White	Black	Total
Under 18	51,688,000	9,285,000	62,389,000
Under 6	15,247,000	2,846,000	18,584,000
Under 3	7,804,000	1,434,000	9,493,000

Source: U.S. Department of Commerce, Bureau of the Census, *Current Population Reports,* Series P-20, No. 349, "Marital Status and Living Arrangements: March 1979" (Washington, DC: U.S. Government Printing Office, 1980), Table 4, calculations by the Children's Defense Fund.

[a]Excludes persons under 18 who are institutionalized or who are married family heads.

Table 2

Number of Families in the United States by Presence of Own Children under 18 and Race, March 1979

Presence of own children under 18	White	Black	Total
With children	26,056,000	3,690,000	30,371,000
Without children	24,854,000	2,215,000	27,433,000
Total	50,910,000	5,906,000	57,804,000

Source: U.S. Department of Commerce, Bureau of the Census, *Current Population Reports,* Series P-20, No. 352, "Household and Family Characteristics: March 1979" (Washington, DC: U.S. Government Printing Office, 1980), Table 1.

Family Structure

Black children are far more likely than white children to live with one parent or with no parent.
- More than 4 out of every 5 white children live in two-parent families; less than half of all Black children do.
- Only 1 white child in 38 lives with neither parent; 1 Black child in 8 lives with neither parent.
- Black children live in families headed by someone other than their parents at rates four times higher than those for white children.

Table 3

Percentage of Children by Age, Relationship to Family Head, and Race, March 1979[a]

Age and relationship to family head	Percentage by Race		
	White	Black	Total
Under 18			
Own child	95.8	84.0	93.9
Grandchild or other relative[b]	3.7	14.7	5.4
Not related	0.6	1.3	0.7
Under 3			
Own child	93.6	71.3	90.1
Grandchild or other relative[b]	6.1	27.9	9.6
Not related	0.3	0.8	0.4

Source: U.S. Department of Commerce, Bureau of the Census, *Current Population Reports,* Series P-20, No. 349, "Marital Status and Living Arrangements: March 1979" (Washington, DC: U.S. Government Printing Office, 1980), Table 4.

[a]Excludes persons under 18 who are institutionalized or who are married family heads.

[b]The child's parents may or may not live with the child, but neither parent is reported as the family head.

Table 4

Percentage of Children by Family Living Arrangement and Race, March 1979[a]

Family living arrangement	Percentage by Race		
	White	Black	Total
Living with two parents	83.5	43.4	77.4
Living with mother only	12.5	41.9	16.9
Living with father only	1.5	2.1	1.6
Living with other relative but neither parent	2.0	11.3	3.4
Not in families	0.6	1.3	0.7

Source: U.S. Department of Commerce, Bureau of the Census, *Current Population Reports,* Series P-20, No. 349, "Marital Status and Living Arrangements: March 1979" (Washington, DC: U.S. Government Printing Office, 1980), Table 4.

[a]Excludes persons under 18 who are institutionalized or who are married family heads.

Table 5

Percentage of Children Aged 6-17 by Family Living Arrangement and Mother's Marital Status and by Race, 1975

	Percentage by Race	
Family living arrangement/ mother's marital status	White	Black
Mother never married[a]	0.2	0.4
Mother ever married (child living with mother)		
Father at home	84.6	57.1
Parents separated	2.5	18.3
Father absent without separation	0.5	0.8
Divorced	6.0	9.7
Widowed	2.1	6.1
Child living with father	1.3	0.5
Child living with neither parent[b]	3.0	7.2

Source: U.S. Department of Commerce, Bureau of the Census, *Current Population Reports,* Series P-20, No. 312, "Marriage, Divorce, Widowhood, and Remarriage by Family Characteristics: June 1975" (Washington, DC: U.S. Government Printing Office, 1977), Table S, calculations by the Children's Defense Fund.

[a]Most, if not all, of the children reported here are living with their mothers.

[b]The mother's marital status is not reported.

Table 6

Percentage of Children Living with Two Parents by Age and Race, March 1979[a]

	Percentage by Race		
Age	White	Black	Total
Under 3	86.8	40.8	79.7
3 - 5	84.9	42.4	78.2
6 - 9	83.9	43.0	77.7
10 - 13	82.9	45.1	77.2
14 - 17	80.9	44.5	75.6
Total under 18	83.5	43.4	77.4

Source: U.S. Department of Commerce, Bureau of the Census, *Current Population Reports,* Series P-20, No. 349, "Marital Status and Living Arrangements: March 1979" (Washington, DC: U.S. Government Printing Office, 1980), Table 4.

[a]Excludes persons under 18 who are institutionalized or who are married family heads.

Poverty

Black children as a group live in families with lower incomes than white families. This is true for Black and white single-parent and two-parent families and for per capita family income,[47] median family income,[48] percentage of children in families below the poverty line,[49] and proportion of children on Aid to Families with Dependent Children (AFDC).

- The 1977 per capita income of Black families—both intact and single-parent—was about half that of white families.
- The median family income of Black families in 1969 and 1977 was significantly lower than that of white families.
- Black children in two-parent families are almost three times as likely as white children in two-parent families to live below the poverty line.
- There are more white than Black families receiving AFDC, but there are almost exactly as many Black as there are white *children* receiving AFDC; a far higher proportion of Black than white children are AFDC recipients.
- Many of these differences can be explained by the lower earnings of Blacks, particularly Black males. For example, in 1977, the median income for Black husbands was $9,035; for white husbands, it was $13,482.

---

[47] Per capita money income is the total money income received in a year divided by the number of persons in families.
[48] Median family income means that half of all families received less money income in a year than the amount shown.
[49] Poverty level is an income standard—essentially three times the cost of food purchased according to a defined and frugal plan, adjusted for increases in the Consumer Price Index—that varies by size, composition, and urban residence of the family.

One of the most important differences in the experiences of Black and white children and families is the economics of the life cycle. When the mother is young (under 25), Black and white female-headed families with at least one child have similar poverty rates: 64.3 percent for white families, 75.4 percent for Black families. But in female-headed families with older mothers (25-44) with at least one child, the difference widens to 20 percent.

Table 7

Median Income for Families and Unrelated Persons by Race, 1969 and 1977

(in Constant 1977 Dollars)

Year	White	Black	Total
1977	$16,740	$9,563	$16,009
1969	16,190	9,916	15,593
Percentage change	+3.4%	−3.6%	+2.7%

Source: U.S. Department of Commerce, Bureau of the Census, *Current Population Reports,* Series P-60, No. 118, "Money Income in 1977 of Families and Persons in the United States" (Washington, DC: U.S. Government Printing Office, 1979), Table 11, calculations by the Children's Defense Fund.

Table 8

Median 1978 Family Income of Children by Family Type and Race, March 1979[a]

Family type	White	Black	Total
Husband-wife	$20,680	$16,726	$20,305
Female headed	7,606	5,082	6,494
Total[b]	19,213	9,793	18,166

Source: U.S. Department of Labor, Bureau of Labor Statistics, unpublished data from the March 1979 Current Population Survey, calculations by the Children's Defense Fund.

[a]Exactly half of all children live in families with 1978 income levels below the amount shown.

[b]Includes a few male head only families not shown separately.

Table 9

Per Capita Family Income by Family Type and Race, 1977

Family type	White	Black	Total
Husband-wife	$6,008	$3,926	$5,825
Male head only	6,032	3,920	5,359
Female head only	3,809	1,913	3,181
Total	5,797	3,171	5,478

Source: U.S. Department of Commerce, Bureau of the Census, *Current Population Reports,* Series P-60, No. 118, "Money Income in 1977 of Families and Persons in the United States" (Washington, DC: U.S. Government Printing Office, 1979), Table 2.

Table 10

Percentage of Related Children Living in Families with 1977 Incomes below the Poverty Level by Age and Race, March 1978[a]

	Percentage by Race		
Age	White	Black	Total
Under 3	13.0	46.8	18.4
3-5	13.0	44.6	17.9
6-13	11.7	40.4	16.0
14-15	9.6	40.0	14.0
16-17	8.5	37.5	12.7
Total	11.4	41.6	16.0

Source: U.S. Department of Commerce, Bureau of the Census, *Current Population Reports,* Series P-60, No. 119, "Characteristics of the Population Below the Poverty Level: 1977" (Washington, DC: U.S. Government Printing Office, 1979), Table 11.

[a]Children living with a family but related to no person in the household—such as foster children—are excluded. The poverty-level income for a family of four in 1977 was $6,157.

Table 11

Percentage of Related Children Living in Families with 1978 Incomes below the Poverty Level by Family Type and Race, March 1979[a]

Family type	Percentage by Race		
	White	Black	Total
Male headed[b]	6.8	17.6	7.9
Female headed	39.9	66.4	50.6
All families	11.0	41.2	15.7

Source: U.S. Department of Commerce, Bureau of the Census, *Current Population Reports,* Series P-60, No. 120, "Money Income and Poverty Status of Families and Persons in the United States: 1978 (Advance Report)" (Washington, DC: U.S. Government Printing Office, 1979), Table 18.

[a]Children living with a family but related to no person in the household—such as foster children—are excluded. The poverty-level income for a family of four in 1978 was $6,628.

[b]Includes a few male head only families not shown separately.

Table 12

Percentage of Related Children Living in Families with 1977 Incomes below the Poverty Level by Ages of Children in the Family, Family Type, and Race, March 1978[a]

Family type and ages of children	Percentage by Race			
	White	Black	Total
Husband-wife			
Children under 6 only	7.0	17.2	7.9
Children 6-18 only	5.4	15.4	6.3
Children in both age groups	9.9	23.8	11.8
Female headed			
Children under 6 only	55.4	70.7	61.5
Children 6-18 only	29.2	54.7	37.1
Children in both age groups	62.4	74.8	69.0

Source: U.S. Department of Commerce, Bureau of the Census, *Current Population Reports,* Series P-60, No. 119, "Characteristics of the Population Below the Poverty Level: 1977" (Washington, DC: U.S. Government Printing Office, 1979), Table 20, calculations by the Children's Defense Fund.

[a]Children living with a family but related to no person in the household—such as foster children—are excluded. The poverty-level income for a family of four in 1977 was $6,157.

Table 13

Percentage of Related Children Living in Families with 1977 Incomes below the Poverty Level by Age of Family Head, Family Type, and Race, March 1978[a]

Family type and age of head	Percentage by Race		
	White	Black	Total
Husband-wife[b]			
Under 25	11.6	26.9	13.3
25-44	6.5	15.5	7.4
Female headed[c]			
Under 25	66.4	78.2	72.6
25-44	42.4	65.0	51.0

Source: U.S. Department of Commerce, Bureau of the Census, *Current Population Reports,* Series P-60, No. 119, "Characteristics of the Population Below the Poverty Level: 1977" (Washington, DC: U.S. Government Printing Office, 1979), Table 20, calculations by the Children's Defense Fund.

[a]Children living with a family but related to no person in the household—such as foster children—are excluded. The poverty-level income for a family of four in 1977 was $6,157.

[b]In a husband-wife family, the "head" is designated by the person who responded to the interview.

[c]Assumes the average number of children for male-headed families equals that for husband-wife families; the approximation is necessary because of the relatively small sample of Black families.

Table 14

Percentage of Families with 1977 Incomes below the Poverty Level by Age of Family Head, Family Type, and Race, March 1978[a]

Family type and age of head	Percentage by Race		
	White	Black	Total
Husband-wife			
Head under 25	9.9	17.5	10.6
Head 25-44	5.1	10.5	5.6
Female headed			
Head under 25	64.3	75.4	69.0
Head 25-44	34.2	54.0	40.5

Source: U.S. Department of Commerce, Bureau of the Census, *Current Population Reports*, Series P-60, No. 119, "Characteristics of the Population Below the Poverty Level: 1977" (Washington, DC: U.S. Government Printing Office, 1979), Table 20.

[a]Percentages are of families having at least one child under 18. The poverty-level income for a family of four in 1977 was $6,157.

Table 15

Number of Children and Families Receiving AFDC by Race, 1975

Recipients	White	Black	Total
Children	1,717,362	1,514,319	3,419,671
Families	3,830,718	3,793,830	8,120,732
Average number of children per family	2.23	2.51	2.37

Source: U.S. Department of Health, Education, and Welfare, Social Security Administration, *Aid to Families with Dependent Children, 1975 Recipient Characteristics Study, Part 1. Demographic and Program Statistics* (Washington, DC: Social Security Administration, September 1977), Tables 13 and 14, calculations by the Children's Defense Fund.

Unemployment

Black children see unemployment around them far more often than white children do. Yet Black children—especially young Black children—are *also* more likely to have mothers working or seeking work. Black children see their parents face higher unemployment rates. They disproportionately live in families made up of one or no wage earners. And when they work, their parents earn less than white parents.
- Black children are about twice as likely as white children to have at least one parent currently unemployed and about three times as likely to have *no* parent currently employed.
- More than 1 out of every 2 Black children under 6 has a mother in the labor force; more than 3 out of every 5 white children do not (see Table 20).
- The unemployment rate for Black youths is two-and-one-half times the white rate.
- A Black high school graduate has a greater chance of being unemployed than a white grade school dropout.
- The unemployment rate for Black college graduates is almost twice as high as the rate for whites who never went to college and no better than the rate for white high school dropouts.

Table 16

Percentage of Children Affected by Parental Unemployment by Race, March 1979

Unemployment status of parents[a]	Percentage by Race		
	White	Black	Total
At least one parent currently employed[b]	90.4	69.5	88.4
At least one parent currently unemployed[b]	5.7	10.1	6.3
At least one parent currently unemployed and none employed	2.4	6.2	2.9
No parent in the labor force[c]	6.1	24.3	8.6

Source: U.S. Department of Labor, Bureau of Labor Statistics, unpublished data from the March 1979 Current Population Survey, calculations by the Children's Defense Fund.

[a]Parents in the armed forces are counted as employed.

[b]A child with two parents, one employed and one unemployed, would be counted twice, once in each of these two categories.

[c]A parent who is neither currently employed nor currently seeking work is counted as not in the labor force. Most such parents are female heads of young or large families.

Table 17

Percentage of Youths Aged 16-21 Who Are Unemployed by Sex and Race, July 1979[a]

	Percentage by Race		
Sex	White	Black	Total
Male	10.7	26.7	12.6
Female	11.7	29.0	13.9
Total	11.2	27.8	13.2

Source: U.S. Department of Labor, Bureau of Labor Statistics, *Employment and Earnings,* Vol. 26, No. 8 (August 1979), Table A-7.
[a]Excludes students currently enrolled in school.

Table 18

Percentage of Youths Aged 16-24 Who Are Unemployed by Level of Education Completed and Race, October 1978[a]

Level of education completed	Percentage by Race White	Black
8 years or less	17.1	24.7
1-3 years of high school	16.3	30.6
High school graduate	7.0	21.9
1-3 years of college	4.5	16.5
4 years of college or more	5.7	15.1

Source: U.S. Department of Labor, Bureau of Labor Statistics, unpublished data from the October 1978 Current Population Survey, calculations by the Children's Defense Fund.

[a]Excludes students currently enrolled in school.

Maternal Employment and Child Care

The structure and employment patterns of Black families have striking implications for the day care needs of Black children.
- In March 1979, almost 50 percent of all Black children under 6 had mothers either working or seeking work.
- Black women tend to enter the labor force at their maximum participation rate as soon as their youngest child is at least 3, while white women reach their maximum participation rate only after their youngest child is over 6, and then only if a husband is not at home. The result is that more Black children need full-time child care—and at younger ages—than white children.
- While Black and white children attend preschools at almost identical rates (53.1 percent of all 3- to 5-year-old Black children and 49.5 percent of all 3- to 5-year-old white children), almost 60 percent of the Black children enrolled in preschool attend full-day programs; 75 percent of white children attending preschool go to part-time preschools.
- When families use private rather than public preschools, 3 out of 4 Black children are placed in full-time settings, while 3 out of 4 white children are placed in part-time settings.

Table 19

Percentage of Children Whose Mothers Work or Are Seeking Work by Age of Child and Race, March 1979

	Percentage by Race		
Age	White	Black	Total
Under 6	41.1	49.6	42.2
6 - 13	53.0	59.0	53.9
14 - 17	54.4	58.1	57.5
Total	50.7	56.2	51.4

Source: U.S. Department of Labor, Bureau of Labor Statistics, unpublished data from the March 1979 Current Population Survey, calculations by the Children's Defense Fund.

Table 20

Percentage of Children under 6 Whose Mothers Work or Are Seeking Work by Race and Family Type, March 1979

	Percentage by Race		
Family type	White	Black	Total
Husband-wife	39.5	55.3	40.9
Female headed	58.9	45.0	53.1
Total[a]	41.1	49.6	42.2

Source: U.S. Department of Labor, Bureau of Labor Statistics, unpublished data from the March 1979 Current Population Survey, calculations by the Children's Defense Fund.

[a]Includes a few male head only families not shown separately.

Table 21

Percentage of Children Aged 3-5 Attending Nursery School or Kindergarten by Age, Length of Day, and Race, October 1978

	Percentage by Race		
Age and length of day	White	Black	Total
3 years old			
Full time	7.1	24.9	10.1
Part time	16.4	8.8	15.0
Total	23.5	33.7	25.1
4 years old			
Full time	10.3	29.6	13.6
Part time	31.5	19.3	29.8
Total	41.8	48.9	43.4
5 years old			
Full time	19.1	37.5	22.5
Part time	64.0	38.7	59.6
Total	83.1	76.2	82.1
3-5 years old, total			
Full time	12.2	30.8	15.4
Part time	37.3	22.3	34.9
Total	49.5	53.1	50.3

Source: U.S. Department of Education, National Center for Education Statistics, unpublished data from the October 1978 Current Population Survey, calculations by the Children's Defense Fund.

Table 22

**Percentage of Children Aged 3-5
Attending Nursery School or Kindergarten
Who Are in Full-day Programs
by Type of Program and Race, October 1978**

	Percentage by Race		
Type of program	White	Black	Total
Public	23.2	54.2	30.2
Private	26.5	74.5	31.2
Total (public or private full-day program)	24.6	58.0	30.6

Source: U.S. Department of Education, National Center for Education Statistics, unpublished data from the October 1978 Current Population Survey, calculations by the Children's Defense Fund.

Education

From the very beginning, the odds of succeeding in school are stacked against Black children.
- A Black child is almost twice as likely as a white child to grow up in a family whose head did not complete high school. Conversely, a white child is four times as likely as a Black child to grow up in a family headed by a college graduate, thus reflecting nearly two generations of inferior educational opportunities for Blacks.
- One Black and white child in every 3 attends a racially isolated school, where over 90 percent of the students are the same race.
- Out of some 1,264,000 American children aged 7 to 17 who were not enrolled in any school in 1976, 172,000 were Black. One out of every 13 Black 16- to 17-year-olds was out of school.
- Black elementary and secondary school children are placed in programs for the mentally retarded at more than three times the rates for white children. If the placement rates for Black children had been as low as for white children, almost 200,000 Black children would have returned to regular classes or more appropriate special classes in the 1976-77 school year.
- Of all the Black children in special education programs, over 40 percent are in classes for the educable mentally retarded (EMR). Less than 20 percent of all white children in special education programs are in EMR classes. Except for the EMR programs, Black and white children are placed in special education programs at about the same rates. In fact, EMR accounts for all except 8,000 of the 168,000 Black children placed in special education programs in excess of white rates.

- Black children are suspended from school at twice the rate for white children. Furthermore, the suspension rates for both Black and white students have increased, so that in 1977-78, 3.6 percent of all white students and 7.8 percent of all Black students were suspended. Over half a million of the 1.8 million students suspended were Black.
- Black children scored fewer correct answers than white children at every age in every subject, according to the National Assessment of Educational Progress. The older Black children are, the worse they do.
- For every 2 Black students who graduate from high school, 1 drops out; 1 white student drops out for every 4 who graduate.
- While many Black students stay in school well beyond the normal school age, they still drop out before completing high school. Whites, on the other hand, reenroll and finish high school at much higher rates than do Blacks.

Table 23

Percentage of Children by Family Type, Education of Family Head, and Race, March 1978

Family type and education of family head	Percentage by Race		
	White	Black	Total
Husband-wife			
Not high school graduate	24.3	43.0	25.9
Not college graduate[a]	53.4	49.9	52.8
College graduate	22.4	7.1	21.3
Female headed			
Not high school graduate	37.0	55.6	43.9
Not college graduate[a]	55.4	42.6	50.5
College graduate	7.7	1.8	5.6
Total[b]			
Not high school graduate	25.9	48.8	29.0
Not college graduate[a]	53.6	46.6	52.4
College graduate	20.5	4.6	18.6

Source: U.S. Department of Commerce, Bureau of the Census, *Current Population Reports,* Series P-20, No. 340, "Household and Family Characteristics: March 1978" (Washington, DC: U.S. Government Printing Office, 1979), Table 8, calculations by the Children's Defense Fund.

[a] Includes both high school graduates only and those with some college schooling.

[b] Includes a few male head only families not shown separately.

Table 24

Percentage of Black Public School Students Attending Majority Black Schools by Racial Composition of School and School Year[a]

Racial composition of school	Percentage by School Year			
	1970-71	1972-73	1974-75	1976-77
99 - 100 percent Black	24.17	20.51	19.48	17.94
90 - 99 percent Black	16.57	15.15	14.31	13.97
50 - 89 percent Black	25.24	26.41	27.02	28.14
Under 50 percent Black	34.02	37.93	39.19	39.95

Source: U.S. Department of Education, Office for Civil Rights, "Distribution of Students by Racial/Ethnic Composition of Schools 1970-1976, Volume I: Users' Guide and National and Regional Summaries," August 1978 (processed), calculations by the Children's Defense Fund.

[a]Data are for 1,910 school districts covering 88.5 percent of all enrolled Black students (in 1976) for school years 1970-71, 1972-73, 1974-75, and 1976-77. "Black" in this table excludes children of Hispanic origin.

Table 25

Percentage of Public School Students Attending Schools with Enrollments of 90 Percent or More Same-race Students by Region and Race, School Year 1976-77[a]

Region	Percentage of Public School Enrollment White	Black	Percentage of Students Attending 90 Percent or More Same-race Schools White	Black
Nationwide	60.2	28.8	35.38	31.91
Northeast	45.9	35.7	37.76	29.93
Border and DC	66.3	30.9	50.35	40.91
South	62.0	31.1	27.66	21.50
Midwest	59.0	35.4	48.42	55.91
West	63.6	11.9	36.65	28.86

Source: U.S. Department of Education, Office for Civil Rights, "Distribution of Students by Racial/Ethnic Composition of Schools 1970-1976, Volume I: Users' Guide and National and Regional Summaries," August 1978 (processed), calculations by the Children's Defense Fund.

[a]Data are for 1,910 school districts enrolling 88.5 percent of the nation's Black students. "White" and "Black" in this table exclude children of Hispanic origin.

Table 26

Percentage of Children Aged 5-17 Enrolled in Lower Grades than Typical for Their Age by Age, Family Income, and Race, October 1976

Age and family income	Percentage by Race		
	White	Black	Total
5-13			
Below poverty level	9.3	8.7	9.2
Above poverty level	3.5	6.0	3.8
Total	4.1	7.1	4.6
14-17			
Below poverty level	19.7	22.6	21.1
Above poverty level	8.0	13.4	8.6
Total	8.9	16.6	10.0

Source: U.S. Department of Commerce, Bureau of the Census, *Current Population Reports,* Series P-20, No. 337, "Relative Progress of Children in School: 1976" (Washington, DC: U.S. Government Printing Office, 1979), Table 5.

Table 27

Additional Percentage of Black Students Who Miss Questions on Academic Achievement Tests by Subject and Age, 1971-1975[a]

	Age of Student		
Subject	9	13	17
Reading	13.5	16.7	19.2
Mathematics	15.1	22.0	23.5
Science	16.5	20.1	12.5
Social studies	14.9	14.5	16.0
Career and occupational development	17.4	22.3	18.2

Source: U.S. Department of Health, Education, and Welfare, National Center for Education Statistics, *National Assessment of Educational Progress,* Report No. BR-2, "Hispanic Student Achievement in Five Learning Areas: 1971-1975" (Washington, DC: U.S. Government Printing Office, May 1977), Tables F-1 to F-3 and G-1 to G-3, calculations by the Children's Defense Fund.

[a]The figures shown are the percentages of Black students over and above the percentages of white students who missed an achievement test question, averaged across all questions. For example, an average of 13.5 percent more Black than white students aged 9 missed questions on the standardized reading test. Each of the achievement tests was conducted and administered as part of the National Assessment of Educational Progress. "White," used here, does not include Hispanic students.

Table 28

Percentage of Public School Students in Special Education Placements by Type of Placement and Race, Fall 1978

	Percentage by Race		
Type of placement	White[a]	Black	Total
Educable mentally retarded	1.1	3.5	1.5
Trainable mentally retarded	0.2	0.4	0.2
Specific learning disability	2.3	2.3	2.3
Emotionally disturbed	0.3	0.5	0.3
Speech impaired	2.1	1.9	2.0
Total, above disabilities	6.0	8.6	6.4
Gifted and talented	2.1	1.3	2.0

Source: U.S. Department of Education, Office for Civil Rights, "Preliminary Data Taken from Fall 1978 Elementary and Secondary School Civil Rights Survey: State and National Summaries," November 14, 1979 (processed, revised), calculations by the Children's Defense Fund.

[a]Does not include Hispanic students.

Table 29

Ratios among Public School Special Education Placements by Race, Fall 1978

Placement ratio	White[a]	Black	Total
Educable mentally retarded placements per 100 specific learning disability placements	46.6	155.3	62.3
Educable mentally retarded placements per 100 trainable mentally retarded placements	546.0	876.3	625.3
Educable mentally retarded placements per 100 gifted and talented placements	50.9	272.8	73.4

Source: U.S. Department of Education, Office for Civil Rights, "Preliminary Data Taken from Fall 1978 Elementary and Secondary School Civil Rights Survey: State and National Summaries," November 14, 1979 (processed, revised), calculations by the Children's Defense Fund.

[a]Does not include Hispanic students.

Table 30

Percentage of Public Elementary and Secondary School Students Disciplined during the 1977-78 School Year by Type of Disciplinary Action and Race, Fall 1978

	Percentage by Race		
Type of disciplinary action	**White**[a]	**Black**	**Total**
Suspension	3.6	7.8	4.3
Expulsion	0.5	0.7	0.5
Corporal punishment	3.0	6.2	3.4

Source: U.S. Department of Education, Office for Civil Rights, "Preliminary Data Taken from Fall 1978 Elementary and Secondary School Civil Rights Survey: State and National Summaries," November 14, 1979 (processed, revised), calculations by the Children's Defense Fund.

[a]Excludes Hispanic students.

Table 31

Percentage of Youths Aged 18-24 by Age, High School Enrollment Status, and Race, October 1978

	Percentage by Race		
Age and high school enrollment status	White	Black	Total
18-19			
High school graduate	76.3	55.0	73.5
Enrolled in high school	8.1	20.8	9.8
Not in school[a]	15.6	24.2	16.7
20-21			
High school graduate	84.6	72.6	82.9
Enrolled in high school	0.8	2.2	1.1
Not in school[a]	14.6	25.2	16.0
22-24			
High school graduate	85.6	74.2	84.3
Enrolled in high school	0.4	1.3	0.5
Not in school[a]	14.0	24.5	15.2

Source: U.S. Department of Commerce, Bureau of the Census, *Current Population Reports,* Series P-20, No. 346, "School Enrollment—Social and Economic Characteristics of Students: October 1978" (Washington, DC: U.S. Government Printing Office, 1979), Table 1, calculations by the Children's Defense Fund.

[a]Does not include high school graduates.

Table 32

Number of School Dropouts and High School Graduates Aged 16-24 by Race, 1977-78

	White	Black	Total
Dropouts[a]	640,000	172,000	822,000
High school graduates	2,747,000	347,000	3,161,000
Dropouts per 100 graduates per year	23.3	49.6	26.1

Source: U.S. Department of Labor, Bureau of Labor Statistics Press Release USDL 79-90, "Employment Situation Improved for School-Aged Youth," February 5, 1979, calculations by the Children's Defense Fund.

[a]There were an additional 72,000 dropouts 14 and 15 years old.

Table 33

Percentage of Children and Youths Aged 5-19 Not Enrolled in School by Age and Race, October 1978

	Percentage by Race		
Age	White	Black	Total
5-6	4.6	6.1	4.7
7-9	0.7	0.5	0.7
10-13	1.0	1.1	1.0
14-15[a]	1.6	1.5	1.6
16-17[a]	9.1	7.3	8.8
18-19[a]	15.6	24.2	16.7
Total, 5-19[a]	5.1	5.9	5.2

Source: U.S. Department of Commerce, Bureau of the Census, *Current Population Reports,* Series P-20, No. 346, "School Enrollment—Social and Economic Characteristics of Students: October 1978" (Washington, DC: U.S. Government Printing Office, 1979), Table 1, calculations by the Children's Defense Fund.

[a]Excludes youths who graduated from high school.

Table 34

College Enrollment among Youths Aged 20-21 by Race, October 1978

	White	Black	Total
Percentage of high school graduates in age group	34.1	32.2	34.1
Percentage of total age group	28.8	23.4	28.4

Source: U.S. Department of Commerce, Bureau of the Census, *Current Population Reports,* Series P-20, No. 346, "School Enrollment—Social and Economic Characteristics of Students: October 1978" (Washington, DC: U.S. Government Printing Office, 1979), Table 1, calculations by the Children's Defense Fund.

Child Health

From before birth through childhood and adolescence, Black children suffer from more health problems, yet receive fewer health services, than white children.
- Black women receive less prenatal care—and receive it later in their pregnancies—than white women. Even though prenatal care has been shown to be one of the most important factors influencing infant mortality and health, at almost every stage of pregnancy, twice as many Black as white women lack prenatal care.
- Nonwhite children have an infant mortality rate almost twice that of white children. Although the rates for both groups of children have been declining steadily, at the present rate of change, nonwhite rates will never fall as low as white rates until the white rates reach zero.
- Nonwhite children and teenagers die from illnesses at rates at least 25 percent higher than those for white children and teenagers. Nonwhite youths were found to have tuberculosis in 1974 at a rate more than five times that for white youths.
- Black children lag substantially behind white children in terms of basic immunization rates.
- Black children and youths are treated for mental health problems at higher rates than whites but are far more likely to be institutionalized for their mental health problems than are whites, who are treated more often on an outpatient basis.
- Nonwhite children are twice as likely as white children to have no regular source of medical care. Nonwhite children are five times more likely to have to depend upon hospital outpatient or emergency room services than are white children.
- Nonwhite children are twice as likely as white children to lack private health insurance coverage. Differences persist even within income groups.
- Black children visit a dentist only once for every two-and-one-half times white children visit a dentist.

Table 35

Percentage of Live Births by Month in Which Prenatal Care Began and by Race, 1978

Prenatal care	Percentage by Race		
	White	Black	Total
No prenatal care[a]	1.1	2.9	1.4
Care during last 3 months[a]	3.4	6.4	4.0
Care during middle 3 months[a]	17.3	30.5	19.7
Care during first 3 months[a]	78.2	60.2	74.9
Fewer than 5 prenatal medical visits[b]	5.4	15.2	7.2

Source: U.S. Department of Health and Human Services, National Center for Health Statistics, *Monthly Vital Statistics Report*, Vol. 29, No. 1, Supplement, "Final Natality Statistics, 1978" (Hyattsville, MD: National Center for Health Statistics, April 28, 1980), Tables 19 and 20, calculations by the Children's Defense Fund.

[a]Data exclude New Mexico, which did not report.

[b]Data exclude Maryland, New Mexico, and Texas, which did not report.

Table 36

Infant Death Rates in 1950 and 1978 by Race

(Deaths per 1,000 Infants under 1 Year)

Year	White	Nonwhite	Total
1978[a]	12.0	24.5	14.2
1950	29.9	53.7	33.0
Proportionate decline in 28 years	59.9%	54.4%	57.0%

Source: U.S. Department of Health, Education, and Welfare, National Center for Health Statistics, *Monthly Vital Statistics Report,* Vol. 27, No. 13, "Annual Summary for the United States, 1978: Births, Deaths, Marriages, and Divorces" (Hyattsville, MD: National Center for Health Statistics, August 13, 1979), Table 6, calculations by the Children's Defense Fund.

[a]Data are preliminary and subject to revision by the collecting agency.

Table 37

Teenaged Childbearing Rates by Mother's Age and Race, 1975

(Births per 1,000 Women in Age Group)

Age	White	Black	Total
10-14	0.6	5.1	1.3
15-17	28.3	86.6	36.6
18-19	74.4	156.0	85.7

Source: U.S. Department of Health, Education, and Welfare, National Center for Health Statistics, *Monthly Vital Statistics Report,* Vol. 26, No. 5, Supplement, "Teenage Childbearing: United States, 1966-75" (Hyattsville, MD: National Center for Health Statistics, September 8, 1977), Table 1.

Table 38

Percentage of Live Births Whose Mothers Were Teenaged at Time of Birth by Race, 1975

	White	Black	Total
Percentage of live births with teenaged mothers	16.3	32.9	18.9

Source: U.S. Department of Health, Education, and Welfare, National Center for Health Statistics. *Vital Statistics of the United States, 1975, Vol. I, Natality* (Washington,DC: U.S. Government Printing Office, 1978), Table 1-53, calculations by the Children's Defense Fund.

Table 39

Percentage of Illegitimate Live Births to Teenaged Mothers by Mother's Education, Age, and Race, 1975

Mother's education and age	Percentage by Race		
	White	Black	Total
All teenaged mothers			
15-17	33.0	87.4	51.4
18-19	17.2	67.6	29.8
Mothers who have not entered high school			
15-17	13.3	10.9	12.5
18-19	6.0	4.2	5.6

Source: U.S. Department of Health, Education, and Welfare, National Center for Health Statistics, *Monthly Vital Statistics Report,* Vol. 26, No. 5, Supplement, "Teenage Childbearing: United States, 1966-75" Hyattsville, MD: National Center for Health Statistics, September 8, 1977), Tables 6 and 8.

Table 40

Children's Death Rates by Age and Race, 1975[a]

(Deaths per 100,000 Children in Age Group)

Age	White	Nonwhite	Total
Under 1	1,413.0	2,765.3	1,641.0
1 - 4	37.0	54.5	40.1
5 - 14	15.6	19.6	16.1
15 - 19	24.9	38.1	26.9

Source: U.S. Department of Health, Education, and Welfare, National Center for Health Statistics, *Health, United States, 1976-1977* (Washington, DC: U.S. Government Printing Office, 1977), Tables 26, 27, and 28, calculations by the Children's Defense Fund.

[a]Except for children under 1, excludes accidents, homicides, and suicide.

Table 41

Death Rates of Children Aged 15-19 by Cause of Death, Sex, and Race, 1975

(Deaths per 100,000 Children Aged 15-19)

Cause	White Male	Nonwhite Male	White Female	Nonwhite Female
Cancer	7.1	6.6	5.1	4.3
Congenital	1.7	2.9	1.5	0.9
Heart	2.2	4.4	1.2	3.3
Accident				
Automobile	62.5	28.3	20.8	8.9
Other	30.8	37.5	5.6	7.3
All other	19.0	29.8	11.9	24.0
Total	123.3	109.5	46.1	48.7

Source: U.S. Department of Health, Education, and Welfare, National Center for Health Statistics, *Health, United States, 1976-1977* (Washington, DC: U.S. Government Printing Office, 1977), Table 28, calculations by the Children's Defense Fund.

Table 42

Percentage of Children Aged 1-4 and 5-9 Living in U.S. Central Cities Who Are Not Immunized against Major Preventable Diseases by Disease, Age, and Race, 1978

	Percentage by Race		
Disease and age	White	Nonwhite	Total
Polio (3 doses)			
1-4	36.2	60.7	44.6
5-9	25.6	41.5	31.1
Diphtheria-tetanus-pertussis (3 doses)			
1-4	33.5	51.7	39.7
5-9	24.5	40.0	29.9
Measles (infection or vaccine or both)			
1-4	35.7	45.8	39.1
5-9	23.8	30.5	26.1
Rubella (infection or vaccine or both)			
1-4	34.5	45.4	38.2
5-9	19.0	28.8	22.4
Mumps			
1-4	47.7	59.9	51.9
5-9	38.2	48.1	41.8

Source: U.S. Department of Health, Education, and Welfare, Center for Disease Control, *Preliminary Report: U.S. Immunization Survey, 1978* (Atlanta, GA: Public Health Service, 1980), Tables 10, 11, 12, 13, and 14, calculations by the Children's Defense Fund.

Table 43

Percentage of Children with Nutritional Intake below Established Standards by Nutrient, Age, and Race, 1971-1974

Nutrient and children's age[a]	Percentage by Race		
	White	Black	Total
Protein			
1	2.7	6.5	3.5
2-5	4.6	7.9	5.0
6-11	5.5	12.0	6.5
12-17	34.7	42.5	35.6
Calcium			
1	10.3	27.6	13.4
2-5	13.4	30.6	16.0
6-11	10.9	21.7	12.5
12-17	24.1	42.2	26.4
Iron			
1	93.2	95.8	93.7
2-5	83.7	80.4	83.2
6-11	58.0	64.1	58.8
12-17	77.5	84.4	78.4
Vitamin A			
1	24.7	41.9	27.5
2-5	33.6	42.2	34.7
6-11	34.2	47.9	36.3
12-17	56.7	67.3	57.9

Source: U.S. Department of Health, Education, and Welfare, National Center for Health Statistics, *Vital and Health Statistics,* Series 11, No. 209, "Caloric and Selected Nutrient Values for Persons 1-74 Years of Age: First Health and Nutrition Examination Survey, United States, 1971-1974" (Hyattsville, MD: National Center for Health Statistics, June 1979), Tables 7, 8, 9, 10, and 11, calculations by the Children's Defense Fund.

[a]Standardized to uniform age and sex distribution within races by the Children's Defense Fund.

Table 44

Percentage of Children Who Eat Specific Food Groups Less Frequently than Once a Day by Age and Race, 1971-1974

	Percentage by Race		
Age and food group	White	Black	Total
1 - 5			
Milk	13.6	15.8	14.1
Meat and poultry	14.2	16.1	14.5
Fruits and vegetables	7.5	13.4	8.3
Desserts	40.4	42.3	40.7
6 - 11			
Milk	9.8	20.5	11.3
Meat and poultry	11.4	10.1	11.2
Fruits and vegetables	6.4	10.4	7.0
Desserts	36.2	40.3	36.8
12 - 17			
Milk	22.3	30.6	23.4
Meat and poultry	15.0	14.7	14.9
Fruits and vegetables	9.9	19.5	11.2
Desserts	51.7	53.0	51.9

Source: U.S. Department of Health, Education, and Welfare, National Center for Health Statistics, *Advanced Data*, No. 21, "Selected Findings: Food Consumption Profiles of White and Black Persons 1-74 Years of Age in the United States, 1971-74" (Hyattsville, MD: National Center for Health Statistics, June 26, 1978), Tables 4, 5, and 6, calculations by the Children's Defense Fund.

Table 45

Rate of Newly Detected Active Tuberculosis Cases by Age, Sex, and Race, 1974

(Cases per 100,000 Children in Age Group)

Age	White Male	Nonwhite Male	White Female	Nonwhite Female
5-14	1.3	8.4	1.7	9.0
15-24	3.8	21.0	3.8	21.6

Source: U.S. Department of Health, Education, and Welfare, Center for Disease Control, *Tuberculosis in the United States, 1974* (Atlanta, GA: Public Health Service, 1977), Table 3.

Table 46

Percentage of Children under 15 by Source of Health Care and Race, 1975

	Percentage by Race		
Source of health care	White	Nonwhite	Total
No usual place of medical care	7.5	15.0	8.7
Private office or clinic	55.4	36.9	52.5
Group practice	28.3	20.7	27.1
Hospital outpatient clinic	3.1	16.4	5.2
Hospital emergency room	0.3	1.3	0.5
Other or unknown	5.4	9.7	6.0

Source: U.S. Department of Health, Education, and Welfare, National Center for Health Statistics, *Health, United States, 1976-1977* (Washington, DC: U.S. Government Printing Office, 1977), Table 57, calculations by the Children's Defense Fund.

Table 47

Percentage of Children under 17 Who Have Not Seen a Doctor in the Last Year by Age and Race, 1977

	Percentage by Race		
Age	White	Black	Total
Under 6	10.7	14.8	11.3
6-16	30.3	36.7	31.3
Total under 17	24.3	29.8	25.2

Source: U.S. Department of Health, Education, and Welfare, National Center for Health Statistics, unpublished data from the 1977 National Health Interview Survey, calculations by the Children's Defense Fund.

Table 48

Dental Visits of Children under 17 by Race, 1976-1977

	White	Black	Total
Percentage not visiting dentist in the last year	44.1	64.4	49.4
Visits to dentist per year per child	1.7	0.7	1.5

Source: U.S. Department of Health, Education, and Welfare, National Center for Health Statistics, *Health, United States, 1979* (Hyattsville, MD: National Center for Health Statistics, prepublication copy, undated, issued April 1980), Table 2 of Part A, calculations by the Children's Defense Fund.

Table 49

Percentage of the Population under 17 Lacking Private Hospital and Surgical Insurance Coverage by Family Income and Race, 1974

Percentage by Race and Type of Coverage

Family income	White Hospital	Nonwhite Hospital	White Surgical	Nonwhite Surgical
Under $5,000	67.8	78.4	68.6	79.8
$5,000 - $9,999	32.9	46.0	34.1	47.4
$10,000 or more	8.3	13.0	9.3	14.4
All income levels	19.6	46.8	20.6	48.1

Source: U.S. Department of Health, Education, and Welfare, National Center for Health Statistics, *Vital and Health Statistics,* Series 10, No. 117, "Hospital and Surgical Insurance Coverage, United States—1974" (Hyattsville, MD: National Center for Health Statistics, August 1977), Table 4.

Table 50

Rates of Admission to State and County Mental Hospitals by Type of Admission, Age, Sex, and Race, 1975

(Admissions per 100,000 Persons in Age Group)

Type of admission and age	White Male	Nonwhite Male	White Female	Nonwhite Female
Inpatient				
Under 18	39.3	103.1	23.6	52.2
18 - 24	343.9	892.1	129.4	241.8
Outpatient				
Under 18	620.7	947.3	385.4	480.4
18 - 24	798.3	881.3	965.5	699.0

Source: President's Commission on Mental Health, *Task Panel Reports Submitted to The President's Commission on Mental Health, Volume III, Appendix* (Washington, DC: U.S. Government Printing Office, 1978), unnumbered tables on pages 832 and 833.

Table 51

Drug and Alcohol Use among Youths by Race

Drug, age, and year	Percentage of Age Group Ever Using Drug		
	White	Black[a]	Total
Alcohol, 12-17, 1977	33	23	31.2
Marihuana, 12-17, 1977	29	26	28.2
Heroin, 20-21, 1974-75	7	2	7

Source: U.S. Department of Health, Education, and Welfare, National Institute on Drug Abuse, *National Survey on Drug Abuse: 1977, Volume I, Main Findings* (Washington, DC: U.S. Government Printing Office, 1978), Tables 16 and 76; U.S. Department of Health, Education, and Welfare, National Institute on Drug Abuse, *Young Men and Drugs—A Nationwide Survey* (Springfield, VA: National Technical Information Service, February 1976), Table 2.4.

[a]Except for Heroin, nonwhite.

Housing

Black children are more than twice as likely as white children to live in inadequate housing. One Black child in every 4 lives in inadequate housing; among families who rent, 1 Black child in every 3 lives in inadequate housing.

Table 52

Percentage of Children Living in Inadequate Housing by Family Structure, Rental Status, and Race, Fall 1977[a]

Family structure and rental status	White[b]	Black	Total
Two-parent families			
Owned housing	6.5	12.1	7.6
Rented housing	20.9	34.0	24.4
Total	9.1	20.5	11.4
Female-headed families			
Owned housing	10.4	18.8	12.7
Rented housing	17.1	32.6	27.1
Total	13.8	29.8	22.1
All families[c]			
Owned housing	6.8	13.5	8.0
Rented housing	20.0	33.6	25.4
Total	9.7	24.7	13.1

Source: U.S. Department of Housing and Urban Development, Office of Policy Development and Research, unpublished data from the 1977 Annual Housing Survey, calculations by the Children's Defense Fund.

[a] "Inadequate housing" means a dwelling unit lacking one or more of the following: plumbing, kitchen, sewage system, heating (except in the South), access to toilets, or physical or electrical maintenance to a degree that threatens health or safety.

[b] Excludes Hispanics.

[c] Includes a few male head only families.

Children Without Homes

Black children are more likely than white children to live without or away from their families.
- Black children under 18 live with nonrelatives or in informal group quarters at three times the rate white children do.[50]
- Blacks are disproportionately represented in institutions that typically serve the young: children's homes, psychiatric facilities, and homes for the mentally and physically handicapped. In all of these facilities, the median age of nonwhite residents is 18 or less, while the median age of white residents is generally older.
- Nonwhite male children under 18 live in institutions at rates more than 70 percent above the rate for white males. Nonwhite female children live in institutions at rates about 25 percent higher than those for whites.[51] The difference is most extreme for institutions for mentally handicapped children but nearly as extreme for children's institutions such as group homes and facilities for neglected children.
- Twice as many nonwhites as whites living in institutions have no families: 17.1 percent compared with 8.5 percent, respectively.

---

[50] Informal group quarters include unconventional dwelling units (barracks, nonresidential buildings) and usual dwelling units (apartments, houses, mobile homes) where five or more persons unrelated to the person in charge live together; informal group quarters exclude formal residential institutions such as orphanages, health facilities, and licensed or certified group homes.

[51] Excluded are correctional institutions, most schools, foster families, and short-term care institutions (e.g., hospitals). Included are formally certified group homes, nursing homes, homes and schools for the mentally and physically handicapped, orphanages, homes for dependent children, homes for unwed mothers, and sheltered and custodial care homes.

Table 53

Number of Children Not Living with Relatives or in Institutions by Age, Residential Arrangement, and Race, March 1978[a]

Age and arrangement	White	Black	Total
Under 3 (total)	28,000	49,000	78,000
In households	16,000	29,000	45,000
In group quarters	11,000	20,000	33,000
3-5 (total)	22,000	21,000	48,000
In households	15,000	12,000	30,000
In group quarters	8,000	9,000	18,000
6-13 (total)	100,000	59,000	166,000
In households	69,000	37,000	111,000
In group quarters	31,000	23,000	54,000
14-17 (total)[b]	97,000	28,000	131,000
In households	88,000	18,000	112,000
In group quarters	10,000	9,000	19,000
Total, under 18	248,000	157,000	423,000
In households	189,000	96,000	299,000
In group quarters	60,000	60,000	124,000
Percentage under 18	0.5	1.7	0.7
In households	0.4	1.0	0.5
In group quarters	0.1	0.6	0.2

Source: U.S. Department of Commerce, Bureau of the Census, *Current Population Reports,* Series P-20, No. 338, "Marital Status and Living Arrangements: March 1978" (Washington, DC: U.S. Government Printing Office, 1979), Tables 2 and 3, calculations by the Children's Defense Fund.

[a]Detail may not add to totals because of rounding.

[b]Contains a few young college students living off campus away from home and young workers living in boarding houses.

Table 54

Persons in Institutions: Median Age and Length of Stay by Type of Institution and Race, Spring 1976[a]

Type of institution	Median Age (in Years) Nonwhite	Median Age (in Years) White	Median Stay (in Months) Nonwhite	Median Stay (in Months) White
Children's institution	14	14	7	14
Facility for the mentally handicapped	17	29	65	107
Facility for the physically handicapped	17	19	69	35
Psychiatric institution	18	24	6	7

Source: U.S. Department of Commerce, Bureau of the Census, *Current Population Reports,* Series P-23, No. 69, "1976 Survey of Institutionalized Persons: A Study of Persons Receiving Long-Term Care" (Washington, DC: U.S. Government Printing Office, June 1978), Table II-A.

[a]The figures in this table are based on counts of all the residents of the institutions, not just children.

Table 55

Children in Institutions by Sex and Race, 1976

	White Male	Nonwhite Male	White Female	Nonwhite Female
Number	63,580	21,820	51,760	12,990
Rate per 1,000 population	2.3	4.0	1.9	2.4

Source: U.S. Department of Commerce, Bureau of the Census, *Current Population Reports,* Series P-23, No. 69, "1976 Survey of Institutionalized Persons: A Study of Persons Receiving Long-Term Care" (Washington, DC: U.S. Government Printing Office, June 1978), Table II-4, calculations by the Children's Defense Fund.

Table 56

Percentage of Disabled Child Beneficiaries of Supplemental Security Income by Type of Placement and Race, 1977

Placement	Percentage by Race		
	White	Black	Total
Parental custody, living at home	70.7	85.6	78.7
Parental custody, not living at home	7.7	5.0	6.7
State custody, living in foster care	21.6	9.4	14.6

Source: U.S. Department of Health, Education, and Welfare, Social Security Administration, *Survey of Blind and Disabled Children Receiving Supplemental Security Income Benefits* (Washington, DC: Social Security Administration, January 1980), Table 3-4, calculations by the Children's Defense Fund.

Crime and Arrests

Black children are more likely than white children to be both arrested and victimized by crime.[52] The arrest rates for both races are high.
- Black children are arrested at almost seven times the rates for white children for the most serious violent crimes and are arrested at over twice the white rates for serious property crimes.
- More than half of all arrests of Black teenagers, compared with more than one-third of arrests of white teenagers, are for serious violent or property crimes.

Nonwhite and white teenagers are, overall, the victims of violent crimes at almost identical rates; the nonwhite rate of victimization is only 2 percent higher than the white rate. But the overall comparison conceals a strong pattern of age and sex differences in victimization rates within each race.
- Nonwhite females are almost 40 percent more likely than white females to be the victims of serious crime throughout their teenaged years.
- Nonwhite males between the ages of 12 and 15 are less likely than similarly aged white males to be victims of crime; the young white male rate is almost 50 percent higher than the young nonwhite male rate.
- Nonwhite and white youths over age 15 are victimized at similar rates.

---

[52] Arrest data are drawn from agencies covering about 80 percent of the total population but a higher fraction of the minority population. Some arrests (less than 4 percent) are of children younger than 11. Nonetheless, the rates of arrests per person aged 11 to 17 are much higher for Black than for white children.

Table 57

Death Rates from Homicide by Age, Sex, and Race, 1975

(Deaths per 100,000 Children in Age Group)

Age	White	Nonwhite	Total
1 - 4	1.6	6.8	2.5
5 - 14	0.8	2.2	1.0
15 - 19			9.6
Male	8.2	47.8	
Female	3.2	14.6	

Source: U.S. Department of Health, Education, and Welfare, National Center for Health Statistics, *Health, United States, 1976-1977* (Washington: DC: U.S. Government Printing Office, 1977), Tables 26, 27, and 28, calculations by the Children's Defense Fund.

Table 58

Arrest Rates for Youths Aged 11-17 by Type of Offense and Race, 1975

(Arrests per 1,000 Persons Aged 11-17)

Type of offense	White	Black
Murder, nonnegligent manslaughter	0.02	0.20
Negligent manslaughter	0.01	0.01
Forcible rape	0.07	0.44
Robbery	0.52	5.63
Aggravated assault	0.74	3.12
Violent offenses (total)	1.35	9.37
Burglary	6.55	14.40
Larceny-theft	11.94	28.28
Motor vehicle theft	1.87	3.37
Serious property crime (total)	20.36	46.05
Other offenses (total)	39.89	51.57
All offenses (total)	61.61	107.01

Source: U.S. Department of Justice, National Criminal Justice Information and Statistics Service, *Sourcebook of Criminal Justice Statistics—1977* (Washington, DC: U.S. Government Printing Office, 1978), Table 4.7; U.S. Department of Commerce, Bureau of the Census, *Current Population Reports,* Series P-25, No. 721, "Estimates of the Population of the United States by Age, Sex, and Race: 1970 to 1977" (Washington, DC: U.S. Government Printing Office, April 1978), Table 2, calculations by the Children's Defense Fund.

Table 59

Rates of Personal Victimization by Serious Crime for Youths Aged 12-19 by Age, Sex, and Race, 1974[a]

(Victimizations per 100,000 Children in Age Group)

Age and sex	White	Nonwhite	Ratio, Nonwhite to White
12 - 15			
Male	3729	2505	0.67
Female	1664	2375	1.43
Total, 12 - 15	2649	2440	
16 - 19			
Male	5540	5786	1.04
Female	2306	3118	1.35
Total, 16 - 19	3906	4397	
12 - 19			
Male	4605	4033	0.88
Female	1984	2735	1.39
Total, 12 - 19	3299	3371	

Source: U.S. Department of Justice, National Criminal Justice Information and Statistics Service, *Sourcebook of Criminal Justice Statistics—1977* (Washington, DC: U.S. Government Printing Office, 1978), Table 3.11, calculations by the Children's Defense Fund.

[a] "Serious crime" refers to rape, robbery with injury and/or with serious assault, and assault with injury and/or with a weapon.

CDF Board of Directors

Lisle Carter (Chairman)
President, University of the District of Columbia; and
Former HEW Assistant Secretary for Individual and Family Services
Washington, D.C.

Julius Chambers
Attorney, Chambers, Stein, Ferguson & Becton; and
President, NAACP Legal Defense and Educational Fund
Charlotte, North Carolina

Marian Wright Edelman
President, Children's Defense Fund
Washington, D.C.

Winifred Green
President, Southern Coalition for Educational Equity
Jackson, Mississippi

David C. Grimes
Chief Executive Officer, Brentwood Savings & Loan Association
Los Angeles, California

Dorothy Height
National President, National Council of Negro Women
Washington, D.C.

William Howard
President, National Council of Churches
New York, New York

Hubert E. Jones
Dean, School of Social Work, Boston University; and
Chairman, Massachusetts Advocacy Center
Boston, Massachusetts

Vernon Jordan
President, National Urban League
New York, New York

Ruby G. Martin
Attorney; and Former Director, Office of Civil Rights
Richmond, Virginia

Joseph L. Rauh, Jr.
Attorney, Rauh, Silard and Lichtman
Washington, D.C.

Hillary Rodham
Attorney, Rose, Nash, Williamson, Carroll, Clay & Giroir; and
President, Arkansas Advocates for Children and Families
Little Rock, Arkansas

Donna Shalala
President, Hunter College; and Former Assistant Secretary
for Policy Development and Research, HUD
New York, New York

Rachel Tompkins
Director, Citizens Council for Ohio Schools
Cleveland, Ohio

Thomas A. Troyer
Attorney, Caplin & Drysdale
Washington, D.C.

Dick Warden
Legislative Director, United Auto Workers; and
Former Assistant Secretary for Legislation, HEW
Washington, D.C.

Nan Waterman
Former Chairman and Member, National Governing Board,
Common Cause
Muscatine, Iowa

Mrs. Andrew Young
Chairwoman, Commission on the International Year of the Child
Atlanta, Georgia

Current Support for CDF

Aetna Life & Casualty Foundation
Avis Rent-A-Car Systems Incorporated
Booth Ferris Foundation
Brentwood Savings & Loan Association
Carnegie Corporation of New York
Celanese Corporation
The Edna McConnell Clark Foundation
Robert Sterling Clark Foundation, Inc.
Exxon Corporation
The Field Foundation
The Ford Foundation
Foundation for Child Development
William T. Grant Foundation
The Joyce Foundation
The J.M. Kaplan Fund, Inc.
Levi Strauss Foundation
Morgan Guaranty Trust Company
 of New York Charitable Trust
Charles Stewart Mott Foundation
The New World Foundation
New York Community Trust—DeWitt Wallace Fund
Charles H. Revson Foundation, Inc.
Rockefeller Brothers Fund
The Rockefeller Foundation
Southern Education Foundation

As a private institution, CDF is grateful for individual contributions to our work.

CDF Publications

Books

Children Out of School in America	$5.00
School Suspensions: Are They Helping Children?	5.00
The Elementary and Secondary School Civil Rights Survey: An Analysis	3.00
Doctors and Dollars Are Not Enough: How to Improve Health Services for Children and their Families	4.00
EPSDT: Does It Spell Health Care For Poor Children?	4.00
Children Without Homes	5.00
Children in Adult Jails	4.00
Where Do You Look? Whom Do You Ask? How Do You Know? Information Resources for Child Advocates	5.00
Portrait of Inequality: Black and White Children in America	5.00

Handbooks

A Child Advocate's Guide to Capitol Hill	2.50
Building a House on the Hill for Our Children: CDF's Children's Public Policy Network	1.50
America's Children and their Families: Basic Facts	1.50
94-142 and 504: Numbers that Add Up to Educational Rights for Handicapped Children	2.00
Your School Records	1.00
For the Welfare of Children	1.50
It's Time to Stand Up for Your Children	1.50
National Legislative Agenda for Children	Free
What Is CDF?	Free
Annual Report	Free

These publications may be ordered from the Publications Department, Children's Defense Fund, 1520 New Hampshire Ave., N.W., Washington, D.C. 20036. Add 10% to the prices above for postage and handling. Bulk discount rates are available: 10-19 copies, 10% off; 20-99 copies, 20% off; 100 copies or more, 25% off. Orders under $10 must be prepaid.

… **Endorsements of** *Portrait of Inequality*

"We have carefully read and been deeply moved by *Portrait of Inequality*. It is the clearest description of the problems and challenges facing poor children that we have encountered during the last decade. The specific action agenda provides the clear goals so badly needed by the Black Church. We stand ready to educate our people, plan joint actions, and vigorously pursue the changes needed in our public policy."

> Dr. Donald Jacobs
> National Director
> Dr. George Lucas
> President
> Partners in Ecumenism

"If there is any lingering doubt about the disparities between the quality of life of white children and Black children in the United States, it has been convincingly put to rest by the *Portrait of Inequality*. Using all the major, universally accepted indices for assessing the well-being of children, CDF gives us more than enough evidence that our society has virtually abandoned one of her most precious natural resources. The data the book provides is by itself an outstanding contribution to our understanding of this national crisis. But as a Christian minister, I am drawn to the excellent and concrete action plan which CDF has also proposed. The next step is mine."

> M. William Howard
> President
> National Council of the
>   Churches of Christ

"This book is the sort of report that shocks but does not paralyze. It is a startling document that stresses programmatic action. Our children need us and we need the sort of guidance *Portrait of Inequality* provides."

> Dr. Cyprian Lamar Rowe, FMS
> Executive Director
> National Office for Black
> Catholics

"Having read *Portrait of Inequality*, I am convinced that it has the kind of information that needs to be disseminated not only in the Black community, but also in the majority population. It is going to take the combined efforts of all people committed to justice and to the liberation of all people—especially Black youth—to alleviate the conditions the book addresses."

> Rev. Vance Summers, Jr.
> Chairperson
> Black Methodists for Church
> Renewal

"I am impressed with the information collected in *Portrait of Inequality*. At the same time, I am saddened by its message: our children are suffering. I think the implementation of the action agenda can go a long way toward solving the many problems that plague Black children and their families across America. I urge members of the Black community to read this important document."

> Rev. Lymell Carter
> General Secretary
> Board of Mission
> Christian Methodist
> Episcopal Church

"I have not seen data of this magnitude as simply written and in as few pages. Although it is painfully shocking, it is must reading for all Americans. We recommend that the Home Mission Board endorse the *Portrait of Inequality* and collaborate with other predominantly Black denominations for the purpose of developing a manual designed for the implementation of the goals and objectives it puts forth."

> Joseph O. Bass, Ph.D.
> Executive Director
> Home Mission Board
> Progressive National Baptist
> Convention

"*Portrait of Inequality* is an excellent account of the myriad problems facing our people today. With feasible and practical recommendations for change that are both short and long range, this is a valuable book for any agency, institution, or individual concerned about making this world a better place for our children."

> Toni Killings
> Associate Director
> Washington Field Office
> Commission for Racial
>   Justice
> United Church of Christ

"*Portrait of Inequality* provides valuable information and an action agenda to accomplish its worthwhile goals. We endorse *Portrait* and support the objectives to which it is addressed."

> John W. P. Collier, Jr.
> Executive Secretary-Treasurer
> The Department of Missions
>   of the African Methodist
>   Episcopal Church

"*Portrait of Inequality* is an extremely valuable piece of work. It accurately documents the deplorable situation our children are in. But it is also hopeful. It not only presents the problem in graphic terms but sets forth an action agenda and goals for corrective measures. This *Portrait* should be read and taken seriously by every segment of the population."

> Kelly Miller Smith
> President
> National Conference of Black
> Churches

"Once again, Marian Wright Edelman and the Children's Defense Fund have cracked the brittle surface that conceals the horrible atrocities being dealt to our children by this society. *Portrait*, in addition to painting a vivid picture of the dismal statistics, is a tool for groups and parents concerned about a step-by-step plan of action to reverse this injustice."

> Shirley A. Small-Rougeau
> Executive Director
> National Hook-Up of Black
> Women, Inc.